*NORTH
PACIFIC
OCEAN*

INDIAN OCEAN

AUSTRALIA

LONELY PLANET'S

BEST IN

TRAVEL

2017

THE BEST IN TRAVEL PROMISE

Where is the best place to visit right now?

This is the most hotly contested topic at Lonely Planet and dominates more conversations than any other. As self-confessed travel geeks, our staff collectively rack up hundreds of thousands of miles each year, exploring almost every destination on the planet in the process.

Where is the best place to visit right now? We ask everyone at Lonely Planet, from our authors and editors all the way to our online family of bloggers and tweeters. And each year they come up with hundreds of places that are buzzing right now, offer new things for travellers to see or do, or are criminally overlooked and underrated.

Amid fierce debate, the list is whittled down by our panel of travel experts to just 10 countries, 10 regions and 10 cities. Each is chosen for its topicality, unique experiences and 'wow' factor. We don't just report on the trends, we set them – helping you get there before the crowds do.

Put simply, what remains in the pages that follow is the cream of this year's travel picks, courtesy of Lonely Planet: 10 countries, 10 regions, 10 cities and a host of travel lists and trending topics to inspire you to explore for yourself.

So what are you waiting for?

28

88

144

CONTENTS

160

196

LONELY PLANET'S

TOP 10
COUNTRIES

Canada / Colombia / Finland / Dominica / Nepal /
Bermuda / Mongolia / Oman / Myanmar / Ethiopia

The Château Frontenac
hotel above Quebec's
Saint Lawrence River

01

CANADA

Bolstered by the wave of positivity unleashed by its energetic new leader Justin Trudeau, and with dynamic cities that dominate global livability indices and a reputation for inclusiveness and impeccable politeness, the world's second-largest country will usher in its sesquicentennial in 2017 in rollicking good health. Marking 150 years since confederation, the elongated birthday party promises to be heavy on bonhomie and highly welcoming to international gatecrashers. And, with a weak Canadian dollar pushing down prices, the overseas visitor should have plenty of pocket money to spend on Canada's exciting fusion food and mysteriously underrated wine.

Population:	36 million
Capital:	Ottawa
Languages:	English, French
Unit of currency:	Canadian dollar

How to get there: Toronto Pearson International is Canada's largest airport; Calgary, Vancouver and Montréal also have big international airports. The long Canada–US land border has numerous road crossings and several rail crossings.

TELL ME MORE...

Sesquicentennial or not, you don't need too many excuses to visit Canada. With vast expanses of barely trammelled wilderness stretched across six time zones, alongside a solid infrastructure and straightforward entry requirements, the country beckons like a giant adventure playground. Among such rugged, uncrowded landscapes, outdoor pursuits, including hiking, climbing and wildlife-watching, are a given. The best way into the country's sometimes forbidding wilderness is via its impressive national-park system, which, in honour of the 150th anniversary, will generously waive all its entry fees in 2017.

Birthdays are also an opportunity to look back and, in 2017, you can review Canadian history in several refurbished museums. Gatineau's Canadian Museum of History is due to open a new wing following a $25-million

> **'Canada...is a relatively young country rich in ethnicity due to the number of immigrants that call it home. Cultural diversity is not only tolerated but embraced!'**
>
> *Tina Varughese, professional speaker*

ITINERARY
Duration: At least three weeks

● Uncover the nation's finest historical heirlooms in **Québec City**, its streets tinged with an old-world European feel.

● Enjoy the best of both worlds in arty, edgy-cool **Montréal**, a glorious amalgamation of Gallic and Anglo flavours.

● See Canada's famous multiculturalism in microcosm in **Toronto**, the country's largest and boldest city.

● Go hiking and spot big fauna in **Banff National Park**.

● Cover all bases in **Vancouver**, set spectacularly amid the mountains and forests of British Columbia – it's home to excellent Asian-fusion food, winter and summer sports, and an anthropological museum replete with myth-invoking indigenous art.

The Jacques-Cartier River in the Parc national de la Jacques-Cartier offers white-water rafting and canoeing fun

MARK READ © ©MARK READ/LONELY PLANET

makeover, while Ottawa's Canadian War Museum will host a special exhibition about Vimy Ridge, the WWI battle won predominantly by Canadian troops in April 1917.

UNMISSABLE EXPERIENCES

• It's practically obligatory for visitors to take in at least one of Canada's 46 national parks and reserves. If your time is limited, hit Banff, nestled amid the Rocky Mountains that straddle the Alberta–British Columbia border; it balances accessibility with the call of the wild.

• For cities, you'd be mad to miss the Anglo-French cultural cocktail of Montréal or the urban-cool-meets-natural-beauty of Vancouver, one of the world's most spectacularly sited metropolises.

• For a real taste of what inspired Canada's bushwhacking European pioneers, pitch north along the remote Klondike Hwy to the Yukon's historic gold-rush town of Dawson City.

TIME YOUR VISIT

Canadian winters are exceedingly cold. Unless you're coming for winter sports, spring and summer are the best times to visit – this is also when the country's wonderful landscapes are most accessible. Canada Day is celebrated on 1 July. Expect 2017's parades, ceremonies and parties to be particularly memorable.

• By Brendan Sainsbury

13

Turquoise Lake Moraine in
Banff National Park in the
Rockies is fed by glacier
water. The area offers great
hiking and skiing in winter

COLOMBIA

Decades of civil war and violent crime meant Colombian passport stamps were once for hardcore travellers only. Fast forward to the present day, and the lost years seem but a dust speck in Colombia's rear-view mirror. There are no world wonders, but the country's mix of vibrant culture, nature and hospitality is a rich tapestry woven by welcoming arms. Over a decade into its dramatic about-face, this South American jewel is even expecting a visit from the world's number-one Catholic. When Pope Francis kisses Colombian soil in 2017, it will mark the Andean nation's first papal visit in 30 years.

The stunning colonial architecture of Cartagena, on Colombia's Caribbean coast, is crowned by its cathedral, finished in 1612

Tayrona Park offers palm-fringed beaches backed by lush mountains. There are even pre-Hispanic ruins in the jungle to explore

Population: 48 million

Capital: Bogotá

Languages: Spanish, English (San Andrés, Providencia and Santa Catalina Islands)

Unit of currency: Colombian peso

How to get there: Bogotá's modern Aeropuerto Internacional El Dorado is Colombia's main international point of entry; Cartagena and Medellín also serve as often-used international hubs. Popular overland routes include via Leticia (from Brazil), Ipiales (from Ecuador), Cúcuta (from Venezuela) and, most dramatically, sailing from Panama via the San Blas Islands.

TELL ME MORE...

Colombia's comeback – partly driven by years of peace negotiations between the government and the FARC (Revolutionary Armed Forces of Colombia), the country's most high-profile guerilla group – is unsurprising considering the country's résumé. From Cartagena to Barichara, it offers some of the most cinematic colonial preservation in all of South America. Towering Andean peaks, lush Amazonian forest and enigmatic, jungle-hidden ruins draw connoisseurs of the great outdoors. Wild and windswept beaches battered by cerulean waters on two coasts lure sun worshippers, whale-watchers and beach bums to its idyllic sands. World-class museums by day and a burgeoning foodie revolution chased by salsa-driven nightlife lure the nocturnally inclined to vibrant cities like Bogotá, Cali and Medellín. But the real coup? The Colombians themselves are a national welcome wagon dead set on inebriating you with a spellbinding cocktail that for decades has been far too seldom served.

ITINERARY

Duration: two to three weeks

Begin in sky-high **Bogotá**, taking in the city's world-class museums and cutting-edge culture.

Head north to the tranquil village of **Villa de Leyva**, a movie set–evoking time capsule of Spanish colonisation.

Spend a few days on the Caribbean coast; begin in **Cartagena** and then linger on less-crowded sands like Palomino or Parque Nacional Natural (PNN) Tayrona.

Beeline back inland to the gorgeous **Zona Cafetera** for a caffeine-fuelled coffee adventure.

Cap it off in Fernando Botero's **Medellín**, where tantalising restaurants and sunrise-shuttering nightlife make for a celebratory send-off.

UNMISSABLE EXPERIENCES

• Wandering the walled Old Town of Cartagena, with its sun-soaked streets, Spanish-built churches and bougainvillea-draped courtyards, brings the fantastical prose of Gabriel García Márquez to life in vivid technicolor detail.

• The multi-day Ciudad Perdida trek deep into the Sierra Nevada de Santa Marta mountains to the mysterious lost city of the Tayrona people is Colombia's most transcendental walk in the woods.

• Be it lobster dinners with the Wayuu people on Colombia's most remote beach at Punta Gallinas or an epic journey to the red-flowing river at Caño Cristales, Colombia's off-the-beaten-path offerings are flooring.

'Colombia is home to the only mountain in the world with snow on top and the Caribbean at the bottom; what's in between is an ecological power nation.'

Simón Mejía, musician, Bomba Estéreo

TIME YOUR VISIT

Excluding the wettest months of October and November, Colombia is fit for fun year-round. It's sunny and dry nearly everywhere from December to February, the whales put on a show on the Pacific coast from July to October, and the Caribbean is bright and blue until May.

• By Kevin Raub

03

Cross-country skiing is a way of life in Finland. Children learn as soon as they can take their first steps

FINLAND

Fought over by Russia and Sweden for 800 years, Finland finally gained independence in 1917. The Finns will celebrate their centenary with gusto, with events planned in every region. Expect everything from al fresco concerts and communal culinary experiences to sauna evenings and vintage-travel-poster exhibitions. There's even a new national park, an 11,000-hectare chunk of land in Hossa, studded with pine forests and crisscrossed with rivers. With the country also playing host to the World Figure Skating Championships and the Nordic World Ski Championships this year, there's never been a better time to discover Finland's proudly unique culture and landscapes.

Population: 5.5 million	
Capital: Helsinki	
Languages: Finnish, Swedish, Sámi	
Unit of currency: Euro	

How to get there: Most flights to Finland land in Helsinki. There are daily ferries from Stockholm, St Petersburg and Tallinn; St Petersburg is also connected to Helsinki by high-speed train.

TELL ME MORE...

Finland shares much of the appeal of its Nordic neighbours, but with its own distinctive twist. Stroll through Helsinki's design quarter to find clean lines, quality craftsmanship, bright pops of colour and quirky patterns. Dip into the New Suomi food scene to discover chefs breathing fresh life into traditional, foraged ingredients and age-old smoking and pickling techniques.

But don't forget to join the Finns in doing what they love best: getting out of the cities and back to nature. Lacking the immediate drama of Norway's fjords and mountains, Finland's landscapes are often left off must-visit lists. Yet the magnetism of the gentler Finnish terrain grows the longer you spend there. More water than land, Finland's patchwork of tens of thousands of lakes, pristine forests, well-marked trails and cosy cabins means it's easy to find your own slice of beautiful isolation, whether bathed in summer's endless light or under winter's frozen spell.

UNMISSABLE EXPERIENCES

• Perhaps it's all that midnight sunshine. Whatever the reason, the Finnish summer brings a bonanza of the world's tastiest berries, from blueberries, cranberries and wild

ITINERARY
Duration: Ten Days to Two Weeks

● Kick off in **Helsinki**, exploring locally sourced menus, design boutiques, and architectural icons, including the rock-hewn Temppeliaukion church.

● Detour to bohemian **Tampere**, where factories have been repurposed as cafes and galleries. It's also home to the newly expanded Moomin museum.

● In summer, boat on **Savonlinna**'s mirror-like waters and enjoy the buzzy opera festival, held in the turreted castle. In winter, discover ice sculptures and long-distance skating along interconnected frozen lakes.

● Finish in **Hossa**'s new national park, canoeing, swimming, hiking and foraging, or snowmobiling and cross-country skiing, depending on the season. The reindeer park stays open year-round.

Discover the joy of foraging
for fresh fruit: Finland's
summer forests yield a
harvest of juicy berries

strawberries to the highly prized cloudberries. Pick up a punnet at Helsinki's harbourside Vanha Kauppahalli covered market or forage for them in nearby Nuuksio National Park.

• The sauna (the only Finnish word to have made it into everyday English) is almost a national religion and is best experienced in your own lakeside cabin, so you can take

'Rauhaniemen is a traditional, lakeside public sauna in Tampere. In summer I picnic on the beach there. In winter, you can still take a dip – they carve a hole in the ice.'

Eliisa Vainikka, researcher, Tampere

a cooling dip afterwards. Search lomarengas.fi for thousands of cottages to rent all over the country.

TIME YOUR VISIT

Independence Day centenary celebrations on 6 December will be rung out with concerts, fireworks and torchlight processions. This is also a good time for Christmas markets, winter sports and Northern Lights spotting. Or, opt for long summer days, when city festivals are plentiful and the lake-quilted countryside calls out for *Swallows and Amazons*–style adventures.

• By Gabrielle Jaffe

LONEROC © SHUTTERSTOCK

DOMINICA

Locals joke that if Christopher Columbus rose from the grave and returned to the Caribbean, Dominica is the only island he would still recognise. One glimpse of its prehistoric ferns and deserted shores, and you'll see what they mean. For decades, an absence of shiny white beaches has helped keep at bay the resort development that has swept through other parts of the Caribbean. Coconut palms are the only skyscrapers you'll see here. Visit before Dominica gets its first large-scale chain resorts in 2018, which will pave the way for a new era of tourism.

04

Soufrière Bay is the rim of an old volcano. The only trace of fire today in this sleepy spot are the hillside pools fed by a hot sulphur spring

Undeveloped Dominica is a haven for wildlife, including the purple-throated carib hummingbird

GYDYTOJAS © GETTY IMAGES/ISTOCKPHOTO

Population: 71,290

Capital: Roseau

Language: English

Unit of currency: Eastern Caribbean dollar

How to get there: Dominica's Douglas-Charles Airport is accessible via other Caribbean islands, including Antigua, Barbados and Puerto Rico; alternatively, take a ferry from neighbouring Guadeloupe, Martinique or St Lucia.

TELL ME MORE...

Dominica's wow factor lies not within its hotels' grounds but outside, where nature sits proudly on her emerald throne. Eco-adventurers whisper Dominica's name as though it's the fabled lost City of Gold, but it's not just the environment that gets fans raving:

it's the Lilliputian guesthouses and locally flavoured boutique hotels; it's pulling up for lunch at a charming roadside shack doling out delicious Dominican comfort food or salty-fresh seafood; and it's mingling with friendly locals, who have quietly picked themselves up and rebuilt after a 2015 storm almost cleaved the island in two. Dominica is the only Caribbean island to sustain an indigenous population of Kalinago, who were all but wiped out by the end of the 16th century elsewhere in the region. A great swathe of Dominican land was bequeathed to the Kalinago in 1903, and ancient myths and legends still hold great sway in their territory.

ITINERARY
Duration: One week

Immerse yourself in Caribbean heritage at **Kalinago Barana Aute**, where indigenous culture is brought to life in the original islanders' backyard.

At **Morne Trois Pitons National Park**, slip into the sublime icy embrace of Emerald Pool, then swim through Titou Gorge for a drenching under its hidden cave waterfalls.

Witness the phenomenon of trapped volcanic air fizzing out of coral-cluttered **Champagne Reef**.

Spy sets used during *Pirates of the Caribbean* filming on a trip down the shadowy **Indian River**.

Explore **Hampstead Estate**, a former slave-run sugar factory, with its evocative 18th-century ruins and gorgeous string of beaches.

UNMISSABLE EXPERIENCES

• Feel your heart beat in time to a pounding waterfall on a rainforest walk along the 115-mile Waitukubuli Trail; its 14 segments are each designed to be tramped in a day.

• Clip-clop right through the partially restored 18th-century garrison at Cabrits National Park – this is an atmospheric horse ride, particularly among the lonelier ruins being devoured by the jungle.

• Take the precipitous hike down to Batibou Beach and pretend you're Christopher Columbus setting foot on an undiscovered Caribbean shore. Dominica's pin-up stretch of sand is blissfully undeveloped, with coconut-strung hammocks, a rickety beach bar and castaway appeal.

'**Dominica is like the Cinderella of the Caribbean... I love its breathtaking scenery, especially the bay in Thibaud and the view of Scotts Head from the peninsula.**'
Jacqueline Douglas, manager, Hampstead Estate

TIME YOUR VISIT

All that rainforest makes Dominica a very wet place, but for the best chance of a warm, golden hello, visit December to May to avoid hurricane season. In May, Hike Fest is an opportunity to get together with other nature enthusiasts to hike the island's trails at weekends.

• By Lorna Parkes

The 5,416m-high Thorung La pass, between Manang and the temple at Muktinath, is well worn by both trekkers and local traders

NEPAL

▬▬▬ **Even natural disasters** can't keep Nepal down for long. The 2015 earthquakes caused devastation, but what is most striking from a traveller's perspective is not how much was lost but how much remains. Landmark temples crumbled, but others came through with just the odd tile out of place, and whole swathes of the country escaped serious damage, including most of the popular trekking trails. Nepal has all the skills required to repair monuments and infrastructure, but what it does need is income. By visiting Nepal now and supporting local culture and people, you could help a nation rebuild and bounce back even stronger.

Population: 31.6 million	
Capital: Kathmandu	
Language: Nepali	
Unit of currency: Nepali rupee	

How to get there: Flights from Asia and the Gulf serve Kathmandu's Tribhuvan International Airport. Many travellers arrive overland by bus from India, particularly via the popular Delhi–Sunauli–Kathmandu route.

TELL ME MORE...

In this part of the Himalaya, disasters come and go, but everything that makes Nepal endures. In Kathmandu and the towns of the Kathmandu Valley, rickshaws still pick their way through cobbled bazaars and temple bells ring out from hidden courtyards. Rhinos and tigers lurk among the elephant grasses in Nepal's national parks, and rugged trails snake through villages of ancient stone houses on the flanks of the world's highest peaks. Even after the disaster, the Kathmandu Valley offers up an embarrassment of architectural riches: soaring tiered temples and palaces, magnificent royal squares, and villages lined with tall brick and timber houses. And wandering around the backstreets of any Nepali town still offers the same timeless tableaux of Himalayan life:

'The whole world knows about the natural wonders and beauty of Nepal, but people forget how special this country is for its people – their genuineness, affability, humaneness and, above all, their unfading positivity.'

Abhi Shrestha, Rural Heritage

ITINERARY
Duration: at least two weeks

- Start by spending a few days exploring **Kathmandu**'s temples and backstreets.

- Next, roam out to Patan, Bhaktapur and the other medieval towns dotted around the **Kathmandu Valley**.

- Pick a trek – there are taster routes lasting just a couple of days, and epic treks to **Everest** and **Annapurna** involving weeks of rugged ascents and descents.

- Celebrate the return to civilisation with a slap-up meal in **Kathmandu** or **Pokhara**.

- Roam down to the plains to seek tigers and rhinos in **Chitwan National Park**.

- Finish your trip by communing with the Buddha at **Lumbini**.

old-timers spinning prayer wheels, grain being winnowed by hand in cobbled courtyards and metal-workers hammering intricate designs into ceremonial pots by the roadside.

UNMISSABLE EXPERIENCES

• Getting close to the Himalaya is the quintessential Nepal experience. You can view the mountains from the rim of the Kathmandu Valley or see the peaks up close and personal on treks to Annapurna, Kanchenjunga and Everest Base Camp. Feeling particularly adventurous? Nepal has a string of trekking peaks above 6000m, as well as serious summits for mountaineers.

• You can connect with Nepal's spiritual side at any elevation. Temples across the country resonate to the chimes of Hindu bells, and Tantric Buddhism fills the air with magic at Lumbini, birthplace of the Buddha, and the towering stupas at Swayambhunath and Bodhnath.

TIME YOUR VISIT

Avoid the summer monsoon from May to September, when rain turns roads to mud, national parks become impassable and clouds obscure the mountain views. Prime time for trekking is October to November and February to April, avoiding the coldest part of winter, when snowfall can block high passes.

• By Joe Bindloss

Annapurna Temple in Kathmandu's Asan Square is dedicated to the goddess of abundance

Lakeside Pokhara offers great food, relaxation and adventure, with three of the world's highest mountains within striking distance

BERMUDA

The British territory of Bermuda is often mistaken for a Caribbean island, and those in the know might not correct the misunderstanding, in order to keep the place to themselves a little longer. Just 1050km off the coast of North Carolina, Bermuda is reachable from most major east-coast US cities in around two hours – a quick hop will get you a bit of Britain mixed with island flair. In June Bermuda will host the America's Cup, where the US will defend its title. Temperate climates and favorable winds make Bermuda the perfect location for this historic sailing race – and for your next trip.

COMSTOCK © GETTY IMAGES

06

Bermuda's more than 34 beaches of azure water and fine white or pink sand are glorious year-round

RUSS HAMILTON © SHUTTERSTOCK

Crystal Cave near Castle Harbour is a 500m walk though geological history with stalactites, stalagmites and deep crystal-clear pools

---

Population: 66,500

Languages: English, either Americanised or British; Azorean Portuguese is also spoken in some older families

Capital: Hamilton

Unit of currency: Bermudian dollar

How to get there: Bermuda's only commercial airport is LF Wade International Airport; some travellers also arrive via cruise line between April and October.

TELL ME MORE...

Bermuda is made up of over 181 islands, islets and rocks, with the eight largest connected by causeways. The cultural influences span Caribbean, West African, Native American,

Portuguese and British – the territory was settled by Brits who got lost on their way to Jamestown, Virginia. This former farming and fishing centre is famous for exports such as the Bermuda onion and the Easter lily, but these days its economy mostly relies on visitors, who come for its excellent golf and tennis, history, pink-sand beaches, and world-class water

'All the colours of my Bermuda shorts are matched to something you will find on the island...the colours of Bermuda are unique. No Instagram filter needed here!'

Rebecca Hanson, founder of TABS Bermuda

ITINERARY
Duration: Two days to a week

Start in **Hamilton:** Front St is filled with boutiques, and notable buildings include the Session House, Ferry Building and Bermuda National Gallery.

Follow the **African Diaspora Heritage Trail,** which takes you through dozens of monuments and museums exploring the Caribbean's slave-trade history.

The World Heritage Site of **St George** can be overwhelming in terms of the number of things to see, but begin with the Unfinished Church, King Sq and the Old State House.

Head underground at the **Crystal Caves**. The blue lagoons and crystal-like walls are almost 30 million years old!

06
BEST IN TRAVEL
2o17

activities such as fishing, snorkelling and diving. Go slow: the official island-wide speed limit is 20mph, and most visitors get around via ferry, moped, taxi or bike. There's also an efficient yet seldom-used-by-tourists bus system; board a bus and you might find it acting as your own private tour coach.

UNMISSABLE EXPERIENCES

• The pink-sand beaches – made from a combination of crushed coral, calcium carbonate and the shells of single-celled organisms called foraminifera – are a huge draw, but exploring the Unesco sites is also extremely popular.

• Gosling's Rum was founded here and is the basis for the island's booziest export, the Dark 'n' Stormy, which is a perfect way to cool down while taking in a cricket match.

• Every month between May and November, tiny glow-worms set Bermuda's waters shimmering.

• All the America's Cup activities will be worthwhile experiences, even if you don't plump for a spectator ticket.

TIME YOUR VISIT
There's something for every water-lover year round, although it's warmest – and most expensive – during late July and August. Whale-watching season is March and April. The America's Cup will be held in June.
• By Lauren Finney

St George's
3

4 Crystal Caves

African Diaspora
Heritage Trail
2

1 Hamilton

Autumn in the Mongolian Gobi, snow-covered Bayan Tsagaan Uul in the distance

07

MONGOLIA

In 2017 Mongolia will raise the curtain on a brand-new capital-city airport, a state-of-the-art facility that symbolises the country's rapid modernisation. Ulaanbaatar has been the biggest beneficiary of the economic boom, its transformed skyline bristling with glass and steel towers. At the centre of this development is a US$500-million Shangri-La complex, which will be completed by 2017, featuring a 290-room hotel, an IMAX cinema and a Hard Rock Café. Beyond the capital lies Mongolia's stunning countryside, highlighted by Lake Khövsgöl, the Blue Pearl of Asia. In 2015 the lake was connected to Ulaanbaatar by paved road, cutting driving time by 10 hours.

Population: 3 million	
Capital: Ulaanbaatar	
Language: Mongolian	
Unit of currency: Tögrög	

How to get there: Mongolia's main port of entry is Chinggis Khaan international airport in Ulaanbaatar, although most flights will shift to the New Ulaanbaatar International Airport (NUBIA) in 2017. The Moscow–Beijing rail link passes through Mongolia, and overlanders can also enter western Mongolia from China's Xīnjiāng province.

TELL ME MORE...

Even as Mongolia urbanises, its main draw remains the steppe and desert scenery, which has changed little since the time of Chinggis Khaan. Nomadic people living in traditional *gers* welcome travellers with fresh cups of *airag* (mare's milk) after long drives. There are opportunities for horseback treks into the taiga to visit reindeer herders or into the Altai Mountains, where Kazakhs still practise falconry. Down in the Gobi, join a hunt for dinosaur fossils or trek across the desert on the back of a two-humped Bactrian camel. In the northern forests, you can join rugged mountain-biking trips or fish for carnivorous Siberian taimen. The winters are brutal, but if you've just arrived on the Trans-Siberian Railway, there are opportunities for

'**Mongolian culture is beautiful. I especially love Mongolian classical and ethnic music, the folk art from western Mongolia, and the drama I feel when watching *naadam* sports.'**
Oyungerel Tsedevdamba, writer and politician

ITINERARY
Duration: One month

• Spend two days in surprisingly cosmopolitan **Ulaanbaatar**, exploring its historic monasteries and excellent museums.

• Spot wild Przewalski's horses at **Khustain National Park** or float down the Tuul River in **Gorkhi-Terelj National Park** on a day trip outside the capital.

• Make a beeline for **Lake Khövsgöl**, Mongolia's natural highlight and the most developed area for tourism, with dozens of *ger* camps and numerous activities.

• Visit the country's extremities: the Gobi Desert in the north, the Siberian taiga of the south, the west's glaciated peaks and the east's verdant grasslands. (Visiting for less than a month? Pick just one.)

A family team competes in Ulaanbaatar's National Day festival and its 'three manly games' – wrestling, horse racing and archery

dog-sledding close to Ulaanbaatar. Chanting monks in ancient monasteries, the haunting music of throat singers and the playful tune of a horsehead fiddler will be your soundtrack along the way.

UNMISSABLE EXPERIENCES

• Giant wrestlers, thundering horses and sharp-shooting archers make *naadam* festivals Mongolia's most visually spectacular events. These 'Nomad Olympics' are best seen in the countryside, where the experience is more intimate and spectators can get closer to the action.

• Those hoping to lose the crowds could arrange a visit with a nomad family. About a third of Mongolia's population remains nomadic, herding their livestock to greener pastures each season. Spending time with a family is not just a photo opportunity but also a hands-on learning experience. Visitors can round up animals, milk a cow or help prepare a traditional meal.

TIME YOUR VISIT

The national Naadam Festival occurs on 11 and 12 July in Ulaanbaatar. Countryside *naadams* fall on this date or later in July. Arrive June to August for the best weather and green landscapes. Avoid winter (November to February), when temperatures plummet to -35°C, and spring (March and April), when dust storms are common.

• By Michael Kohn

41

Gorkhi-Terelj National Park is great for climbers, and you can also hire horses and camels

OMAN

Oman has been the ace in Arabia's pack for a while, but with more flights than ever before and high-end hotels popping up all over the place, the sultanate looks ready to raise its game yet again. Luxury accommodation, including the award-winning duo of Six Senses on the Musandam Peninsula and Alila in the Hajar Mountains, has long had a foothold here, but glitzy properties from Anantara, Kempinski and other high-end names are also slated to open soon. The burst of construction doesn't stop there, though – the US$120-million Majarat Oman, a futuristic theme park for families, is set to debut in 2017.

08

The Sultan Qaboos Grand Mosque in Muscat: commissioned by Oman's ruler and bearing his name, it was inaugurated in 2001

The corniche at Mutrah, one of the largest sea ports of the region and home to the ancient Mutrah Souq

Population: 3.6 million

Capital: Muscat

Language: Arabic

Unit of currency: Omani rial

How to get there: Muscat International Airport is the main gateway, but Salalah International Airport is increasingly well connected. A half-day road trip from Dubai or Abu Dhabi in the neighbouring UAE is another option.

TELL ME MORE...

From its razorback mountains to its shape-shifting dunes, Oman is the stuff of desert dreams. The western Hajar Mountains, which reach their peak at 3075m-high Jebel Shams, are a natural focus of attention for thrill seekers, as are the bronze sands of Sharqiya, where the Bedu people wander among mountains of a different kind.

From Musandam in the north to Salalah in the south, a string of fine beaches scallops the length of the ochre-coloured coast, while smouldering frankincense still perfumes the souks of historic towns like Nizwa and Sur. And then there's Muscat, an elegant, whitewashed, low-rise antidote to other capitals in the region.

In a part of the world that so often seems bling obsessed or strife torn, Oman stands alone as a place that has preserved its charm at the same time as modernising the travel experiences on offer.

'My highlight would be the Selmah Plateau: the view at 1000m from the top back down to the Indian Ocean is breathtaking, as is the steep gravel track you take to get there.'
Eric Walters, founder of Oman tour specialists Hud Hud Travels

ITINERARY
Duration: One week

Enjoy the mystique of **Muscat**, particularly the atmospheric port of Mutrah.

Follow the coast south to **Wadi Shab** for turquoise pools, waterfalls and croaking frogs.

Head inland until you reach a jumping-off point for **Sharqiya Sands**; stay in a desert camp overnight or arrange a mini-expedition with logistical support.

Head north, stopping at the ancient souk at **Sinaw**, then climb to the **Saiq Plateau** for nerve-jangling hikes and uber-luxury retreats.

Return to **Muscat** for a whistle-stop tour of the original old city.

UNMISSABLE EXPERIENCES

Jutting out into the Strait of Hormuz, the rarely visited Musandam Peninsula is eye-popping even by the elevated standards of Oman. Separated from the rest of the country by the UAE, Musandam is called the 'Norway of Oman' thanks to its *khors* (fjord-like inlets) that teem with marine life. If you have time for the side trip from Muscat, exploring the *khors* aboard a dhow (a traditional wooden vessel) as dolphins frolic alongside the boat is not to be missed.

TIME YOUR VISIT

If you can endure the heat of summer, go between mid-June and mid-August to witness the *khareef*, the transformation of the parched jebel hills around Salalah, Oman's second city, as the monsoon turns them into a lush, mist-shrouded oasis of life.

• By James Kay

Bagan, Myanmar's Angkor Wat, is home to over 2500 Buddhist monuments (or their ruins) built between the 11th and 13th centuries

09

MYANMAR

Change has been a long time coming in the nation also known as Burma, but the election of the first civilian government in half a century has all eyes on the future. No one is pretending that all Myanmar's problems have gone away, but things are moving in the right direction, and Southeast Asia's most secretive country is poised to receive an influx of travellers. Visiting comes with challenges, but the reward is a window onto a vanishing Asia, where the difficulties of travel are part of the appeal, and where life moves to the timeless rhythm of chanting monks and monastery bells.

LKUNL ©LKUNLIGETTY IMAGES\ISTOCKPHOTO

Population: 56.3 million

Language: Burmese
Unit of currency: Kyat
How to get there: International flights from Asia and the Gulf serve Yangon International Airport. Flights also run from Singapore and Bangkok to Mandalay International Airport in the north. Buses, trains, boats and domestic flights connect the main cities; note that some areas remain off-limits to travellers or are only accessible by air.

TELL ME MORE...

During Myanmar's long years in the wilderness, visiting at all was controversial. Under the military junta, many travellers boycotted the country as an act of solidary with the Burmese people. Those who did come faced a difficult balancing act in trying to ensure their tourist dollars reached ordinary people and not the pockets of the regime. Challenges remain as the people begin to unpick the tangled legacy of military rule, but the focus is shifting to the wonders of this backwater of Southeast Asia. And what wonders... With more sky-piercing stupas than office towers, Myanmar is home to half the world's old-growth teak forest and is dotted with ruined cities, colonial relics and

'I love Myanmar because people possess such resilience and the desire to change our country for the better. Their generosity of spirit is everywhere, from the daily donations of alms to the warmth and smiles shown to visitors.'

Khin Omar Win, director of Eastern Safaris / Balloons over Bagan

ITINERARY
Duration: Two weeks

- Begin in **Yangon**, the perfect introduction to the Burmese way of life.

- Ramble east to historic **Bago** and the 'balancing boulder' temple at **Kyaiktiyo**, or go west to **Pathein** and the beaches of the Ayeyarwady Delta.

- Next, ride the riverboat north to **Bagan**, which staggers visitors with its more than 2500 Buddhist monuments.

- Follow the Ayeyarwady on to laid-back **Mandalay**, stepping stone to Inle Lake and the tribal heartlands of Shan State.

- With more time to spare, consider **Mrauk U** in the west, or the far south and far north – remote, little-explored places that are only slowly opening up to view.

Myanmar is still a largely agricultural society, barely touched by tourism

©DAVID LAZAR/GETTY IMAGES/FLICKR RF

fascinating tribal cultures. Here the themes of Theravada Buddhism are woven through the fabric of society like the mighty Ayeyarwady River weaves through the rice paddies.

UNMISSABLE EXPERIENCES
Just being in Myanmar is an unmissable experience. This is the vision of Asia that greeted the first backpackers who stumbled along the overland trail: golden temples, tropical outposts, history by the truckload and disarmingly honest locals. When it comes to iconic experiences, Myanmar has a full hand:
- circumnavigating the towering Shwedagon Paya temple in Yangon
- canoeing across misty Inle Lake
- trekking at Kalaw and Hsipaw
- gazing on seas of ruined temples at Bagan and Mrauk U
- taking lazy boat rides along the Ayeyarwady
- mingling with tribal people and trying fresh local food at Kyaingtong's central market

TIME YOUR VISIT
Avoid monsoon season (May to September), when the Ayeyarwady and its tributaries burst their banks and cyclones lash the coastline. The mercury creeps skywards as the first rains start to fall, making for uncomfortable travel conditions, but October to April offers dry skies, warm days and cool nights in the hills.
- By Joe Bindloss

ETHIOPIA

With its own calendar (where else can you get 13 months of sunshine?), timekeeping, script, language, cuisine, church and coffee, Ethiopia is as exotic as countries come. And whether you're trekking through the Simien Mountains to witness wildlife that roams nowhere else on Earth, climbing to a church carved into a remote cliff face in Tigray or boating across the serene waters of Lake Tana to visit an age-old monastery, you'll be overwhelmed by the beauty of the landscape. In 2017 new airline links will make the country more accessible than ever, so be one of the first to hop on board.

DANITA DELIMONT © GETTY IMAGES/GALLO IMAGES

The geladas (aka bleeding-heart baboons) of the Simien Mountains, which is also home to the highest peak in Ethiopia

10

Population: 99.5 million

Capital: Addis Ababa

Languages: Amharic, Oromo, Tigrinya, Somali, Guarage, Sidama and Hadiyigna

Unit of currency: Ethiopian birr

How to get there: International visitors either land at Addis Ababa's Bole International Airport or arrive via the country's operating land crossings with Kenya, Djibouti, Somaliland and Sudan.

TELL ME MORE...

One of the world's great ancient empires, and arguably the first to adopt Christianity, Ethiopia is laden with fascinating historical treasures dating back 2000 years. Take on the easily accessible northern circuit and you can walk in the shadow of centuries-old castles, descend into 4th-century tombs beneath soaring monoliths and gawk at the mystical wonders that are the medieval rock-hewn churches. For a dose of outdoor adventure en route, the Simien Mountains are within striking distance.

Head east to the walled city of Harar, where you can happily get lost in its myriad atmospheric alleys; come dark the brave can feed wild hyenas outside its gates. The south is wilder still, with Bale Mountains National Park and the traditional

'Ethiopia is in my blood. It is my culture and it is the only way I have ever known to live, to speak, to eat, to practise my religion. I love working in tourism to see people learn about my world.'

Frehiwot Alemu, tour company manager

JON BRATT © GETTY IMAGES

Bete Giyorgis (Church of St George) was carved entirely from limestone around 1300, and has been called the Eighth Wonder of the World

10 BEST IN TRAVEL 2017

ITINERARY
Duration: Three to four weeks

Start in **Addis Ababa**, with its rewarding museums, wide selection of hotels and restaurants, and some of the best macchiatos you'll ever sip.

On the shore of Lake Tana, **Bahir Dar** is the leaping-off point for boat journeys to millennia-old island monasteries.

Leafy **Gonder** is home to spellbinding 17th-century castles and palaces.

Trek for two days or 12 in **Simien Mountains National Park**'s epic landscape.

Said to be home to the Ark of the Covenant, **Aksum** is peppered with towering 4th-century stelae and underground tombs (most unexplored).

Finish in **Lalibela**, site of Ethiopia's most spectacular rock-hewn churches.

animist tribes of the Omo Valley.

With such a rich history – one that includes defeating Italian would-be colonisers – Ethiopians are rightly a very proud bunch, but it's their warmth that shines through.

UNMISSABLE EXPERIENCES
• Descend into a medieval world frozen in stone at Lalibela, where 11 ornate churches have been hewn from solid bedrock, to watch incense-wielding priests performing age-old Christian ceremonies – these historical and architectural masterpieces aren't just Unesco-listed showpieces but active places of worship.
• Enjoy a multi-day trek through the stunning 4000m heights of Simien Mountains National Park, where you'll walk amid hundred-strong troops of bleeding-heart baboons (geladas) and search for the perfect picture of an endemic walia ibex standing proudly on the edge of an Abyssinian abyss.
• Witness a Hamer boy become a man in a traditional bull-jumping ceremony in the Omo Valley.

TIME YOUR VISIT
In late September, when the rains end in the northern highlands, the mountains are blanketed with beautiful wild meskel flowers – the following weeks are particularly stunning for trekkers. Pleasant conditions dominate in the north till late May, while in the remote south and Omo Valley things get very soggy between March and May.
• By Matt Phillips

A priest wanders the narrow path devotees must climb to attend services at Abuna Yemata Guh, a cave church perched on a high cliff

LONELY PLANET'S

TOP 10 REGIONS

Choquequirao, Peru / Taranaki, New Zealand / The Azores, Portugal
North Wales, UK / South Australia / Aysén, Chile / The Tuamotus, French
Polynesia / Coastal Georgia, USA / Perak, Malaysia / The Skellig Ring, Ireland

The 16th-century Inca settlement of Choquequirao is free from the crowds of Machu Picchu, but at a price: it's a four-day hike

01

CHOQUEQUIRAO, PERU

Choquequirao, hidden across the deep Apurimac Valley, was the last Inca refuge from the conquistadors, and there's a growing traveller buzz to see it ASAP. A cable car will squeal into life in 2017 (or later; bureaucratic feet are dragging), gliding up to 3000 visitors a day to the ruins in just 15 minutes. Visit in the early days, or take the four-day trek in Inca footsteps, and have a taste of Machu Picchu all to yourself. You'll only encounter a couple of visitors – plus the archaeologists who continue to peel back the jungle, which still cloaks two-thirds of the spectacular site.

Population: 350,000 (Cuzco)
Main town: Cachora
Languages: Quechua, Spanish
Unit of currency: Nuevo sol
How to get there: The main and best-cared-for entry village is Cachora. International flights enter Lima; transfers are available to Aeropuerto Internacional Alejandro Velasco Astete in Cuzco. Buses (including international routes) go to Cuzco's Terminal Terrestre.

TELL ME MORE...

Imagine exploring Machu Picchu before the hordes and mass commerce. A visit to Choquequirao gets you as close as possible to doing exactly that. Sit alone and watch woolly clouds unravel around the fingers of the Andes peaks; watch condors ride invisible currents above the ancient Inca residences; admire the roaring Apurimac River as it makes serpentine twists through the sharp, snowcapped teeth of the mountains; and breathe in the green scent of bromeliads and cacti – this might be your last chance to see an Inca citadel in peace.

Roughly 20 Inca families built Choquequirao where no Spanish conquistadors could find it. If hiking, expect a descent to the Apurimac River, followed by a punishing ascent to the ruins. The reward is seeing Choquequirao carved out of the mountains. The expanse of terraces and

'I love the cultural mix. Andean roots are very present, alive, respected. People go to Mass but then go up a mountain to perform their Andean rituals for their Mother Earth, Pachamama.'
Valentina Rodriguez, Colombian living in Cuzco

ITINERARY
Duration: Six days

Spend your first day in **Lima**, enjoying museums, *ceviche* and pisco.

Next, move on to **Cuzco**, visiting the arty San Blas neighbourhood and adjusting to the altitude. The Choquequirao trek calls for an *arriero* (guide), arranged here or in Cachora.

The following day, set off early on the three-hour drive to **Cachora**, then start the trek, taking in views across the Andes.

On day four, resume the trek, heading across the Apurimac River and up the steep path to Santa Rosa, Marampata and finally **Choquequirao**.

Backtrack on days five and six, or continue on to Machu Picchu.

For five millennia, llamas have been bred by Andean people for their wool and meat, and as beasts of burden

temples so far cleared of its plumage of trees is already as large as Machu Picchu.

UNMISSABLE EXPERIENCES

• Unique to Choquequirao are the stone *llamas blanca* (white llama) figures. Standing taller than most humans, the designs are inlaid into the lower terraces, forming a pattern of animals across the slopes. Run your hands across these white stones clacked into place hundreds of years ago and you'll touch the fingerprints of Incas who built a citadel that eluded detection.

• Clamber back up to the *pampa* (plain) and ascend again for a glorious view: terraces, the green and brown valley, and mountains rising and falling towards the horizon.

TIME YOUR VISIT

Sunny June and July are the ideal times to visit, best synched with a festival in Cuzco. Choquequirao currently closes in the rainy season from November to March, but check for updates when the cable car springs into action. Alternatively, beat the crowds and do the hike, setting aside four days.

• by Phillip Tang

Five hundred years after Pizarro and Balboa, the old Andean culture still thrives in and around Cuzco

TARANAKI, NEW ZEALAND

The joke goes that most travellers who reach Taranaki have just taken a wrong turn, a gag backed by stats showing that just 2% of New Zealand's international visitors venture out this way. But a new motto – 'A Little Bit Out There' – offsets the region's remote location with a deliciously offbeat new gallery dedicated to effervescent kinetic artist, filmmaker, painter and poet, Len Lye. In nearby Egmont National Park, meanwhile, a magnificent hiking trail is emerging from the shadows to challenge the Tongariro Alpine Crossing as the country's finest one-day walk.

SPENCER CLUBB © GETTY IMAGES

Mount Taranaki is the high point of the Pouakai Crossing hike in Egmont National Park

02

Population: 109,608
Main town: New Plymouth
Languages: English, Māori
Unit of currency: New Zealand dollar
How to get there: Domestic flights link New Plymouth with Auckland, Christchurch and Wellington, while all roads in are long and winding.

TELL ME MORE...

The region's geographical and spiritual heart is Mt Taranaki in Egmont National Park, the volcanic cone so damn picture-perfect it stood in for Mt Fuji in *The Last Samurai*. Surrounding it are lush plains and a series of small rural towns, serviced by New Plymouth city (population 74,184). Off Taranaki's wild surf coast are the oil and gas fields largely responsible for the region's perennially buoyant economy.

From dairy farms to legendary surf breaks, the region's natural assets have long been envied. But in recent years a powerful arts and cultural set has elbowed its way to the fore, sustaining New Plymouth's notable Puke Ariki Museum and Govett-Brewster Art Gallery, and one of the world's finest music festivals –

'Glittering air; glowing mountain; hammered green sea: they're obvious.

Ring-plain lifting to inland hills; back-roads tunnels; main-roads artworks: they're special.

Being a country's edge: that's unique – and Taranaki.'
David Hill, writer

Poet's Bridge in Pukekura Park, where the annual WOMAD festival is held

RADIUS IMAGES © GETTY IMAGES/RADIUS IMAGES

ITINERARY
Duration: Three days

● Survey the region from high on Mt Taranaki via the **Pouakai Crossing** hike in Egmont National Park.

● Head to the bright lights of the regional capital, **New Plymouth**, and explore its boutique shopping and dining scenes.

● Visit the **Len Lye Centre** to see, feel and hear art that sways, fizzes, crackles and pops.

● Wander around **Pukekura Park**, a fine municipal garden designated the 'Mayfair' of New Zealand's Monopoly board.

● Head south on **Surf Coast Highway 45** to trace an arc from New Plymouth to Hawera, keeping Mt Taranaki in your sights inland, with endless black-sand beaches accessible down side roads to the coast.

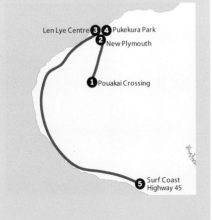

WOMAD – held in pretty Pukekura Park. Now that New Plymouth has its own answer to the Guggenheim – the hard-won and community-funded Len Lye Centre – the stage is set for Taranaki's star to shine.

UNMISSABLE EXPERIENCES

● Don't know your *Wind Wand* from your *Water Whirler*? Wander into the wonderful world of one of the twentieth century's zaniest, most idiosyncratic artists. The new Len Lye Centre adjoining the Govett-Brewster Art Gallery is a shimmery steel *zizz*-fest on the outside, all edgy lines and neck-cricking ceilings on the inside, with a collection of Lye's mind-bending kinetic sculptures and eye-popping films.

● A freshly minted alternative to the overburdened Tongariro Alpine Crossing, the Pouakai Crossing is a day-hike sidling around Mt Taranaki and along the Pouakai foothills. Volcanic, panoramic and arguably every bit as scenic as its rival, its Egmont National Park highlights include Dieffenbach Cliffs, Bells Falls, alpine tarns and primeval Ahukawakawa Swamp.

TIME YOUR VISIT

Visit between November and April to hit Taranaki's black-sand beaches without fear of hypothermia, and linger on the trails of Egmont National Park with ample daylight. To maximise your 'Naki vacation, go during Pukekura Park's Festival of Lights (mid-December to end of January), or mid-March for WOMAD.

● By Sarah Bennett & Lee Slater

The Azores comprise nine volcanic islands in the North Atlantic. This is the Ilha do Pico with its volcanic peak, as seen from Ilha do Faial

03

TOP 10 REGIONS

THE AZORES, PORTUGAL

Blending amazing nature and super-cool Iberian culture, the Azores offer accessibility from North America and Europe without the abundance of travellers who have discovered Iceland in recent years. The 'next Iceland' analogy extends beyond the archipelago's positioning as a fascinating cross-the-pond pit stop. Its natural assets resemble an array of superlative sights pulled from other destinations: lush Hawaiian volcanoes, medieval Portuguese villages, gurgling Scandinavian hot springs, towering Irish cliffs and rugged Patagonian craters. But the secret won't last: the Azores have seen a 31% increase in tourism over the last 12 months, so visit in the 2017 sweet spot before things really take off.

Population: 250,000
Main town: Ponta Delgada, São Miguel
Language: Portuguese
Currency: Euro
How to get there: São Miguel's airport is the major hub for international arrivals – flights are 10 hours from America's northeast, six from London and just two from Lisbon, where travellers can find daily services.

TELL ME MORE...

Settled by the Portuguese around the time of Columbus, the Azores are best conceived of as nine siblings: collectively they feel like a family with many similar traits, but each isle possesses its own character and strength. Big brother São Miguel has all the trappings of big-city living; little Pico proudly pokes its head up to show off a vegetation-furred volcano; long, flat São Jorge lazily unfurls its arable pastures; and Terceira adds a cultural twist, its Unesco-protected villages stocked with chilled-out cafes and independent bookstores. And the longstanding Portuguese influence goes beyond the Iberian charm: Portuguese prices stack up very favourably against those of other Western European countries, and the food-focused culture cherishes all of life's finest: wine, cheese and fresh seafood.

'I love the quality of life, mild climate, and the closeness to the sea and nature. I encourage all tourists to try our seafood – especially limpets and barnacles – and the São Jorge cheese.'

Felipe Rocha, headmaster of the School of Tourism and Hospitality, and São Miguel native

ITINERARY
Duration: One week

• Start on **São Miguel** to appreciate the Azorean version of big-city livin'.

• Puddle-jump over to **São Jorge** for fresh dairy-farm produce and flavourful shellfish.

• Next, take an easy 50-minute boat ride over to **Pico**. Lying under the shadow of its eponymous volcano, it's known as the Black Island for its ash-ridden earth – the rich soil helps sustain several thriving vineyards.

• If you have the luxury of time, add on two more nights on the island of **Terceira** to take in the archipelago's cultural heart: the city of Angra do Heroísmo.

UNMISSABLE EXPERIENCES

• It's all about food and drink on São Miguel. Visit Gorreana – one of Europe's only working tea plantations – for tastings and a trail hike with ocean vistas. Then try *cozido*, a warm stew of meat and veg, slow-cooked directly at the source: a lakeside volcanic field near the appropriately named village of Furnas.

• Paddle Sete Cidades, São Miguel's twin crater lakes; one is a deep blue, the other a brilliant turquoise.

• Hike Mt Pico (2351m), the highest point in Portugal, and gaze across several islands in the archipelago, including Faial, from which the historic harbour of Horta can be seen.

TIME YOUR VISIT

Plan your trip during the summer months – June to September – when the sea is warmer, the native flowers are in full bloom, pods of whales and dolphins can be spotted from the shoreline (especially in June), and the infrastructure is generally more flexible, with increased international flights.

• By Brandon Presser

Angra do Heroísmo on Terceira. Behind the waterfront, the historic centre holds churches, palaces and gardens

MARCO ANTONIO MONTEIRO © GETTY IMAGES

Poço da Alagoinha on Flores, an island named for its rich plant life

RAY WISE © GETTY IMAGES

NORTH WALES, UK

On the site of an aluminium factory in the Conwy Valley, Surf Snowdonia is perhaps the most headline-stealing example of the region's reinvention: the machinery of this inland lagoon generates the world's longest surfable human-made waves. Not to be outdone, Zip World at Penrhyn Quarry boasts the world's fastest (and Europe's longest) zip line. The same folks run Bounce Below: giant trampolines strung in the caverns beneath Blaenau Ffestiniog, one-time capital of Wales' slate-mining industry. Capping things off, Snowdonia National Park – Wales' largest – has been designated a 'dark-sky reserve' thanks to its lack of light pollution. Telescopes out, people (if you still have the energy)!

Llanddwyn Island Lighthouse marks the entrance to the Menai Strait, the strip of sea separating Anglesey island from mainland Wales

04

Festival No. 6 is named after the hero of TV series *The Prisoner*, and takes place where the show was shot, in the Italianate tourist village of Portmeirion

JOHN REES | BLUEISLANDER_OLD / 500PX © JOHN REES / 500PX

Population: 690,000

Main town: Wrexham

Languages: Welsh, English

Unit of currency: British pound

How to get there: In order of distance, Liverpool Airport, Manchester Airport and Birmingham Airport are all close (two hours or less by car, bus or train). Trains from London to North Wales take about three hours.

TELL ME MORE...

Once upon a time the mountains and valleys of North Wales gave up a bounty of slate, copper and even gold; now this landscape, ringed with hills and rich with mythology, is a playground for hikers, mountain bikers and rock climbers. However you get your kicks, you'll work up an appetite – and that's not a problem, as North Wales has also become a haunt of in-the-know foodies. The opening of the Bodnant Welsh Food Centre in 2012 kick-started something special here: gourmet-pleasing annual festivals include the Gwledd Conwy Feast, the Menai Seafood Festival, the Beaumaris Food Festival and more. At Menai Bridge, cult restaurant Sosban and The Old Butchers has such a following that the waiting list runs to

ITINERARY
Duration: One week

From Llandudno, explore **Great Orme**, then take a side trip to Unesco-listed Conwy Castle or perfect your carving at Surf Snowdonia.

Brave the world's zippiest zip line at **Bethesda**, cross the Menai Strait to Halen Môn's new visitor centre, then stroll part of the 200km **Isle of Anglesey Coastal Path**.

Recall the age of steam on the Welsh Highland Railway from **Caernarfon** to **Porthmadog**, the jumping-off point for architectural oddity Portmeirion.

Catch the narrow-gauge railway to bleakly beautiful **Blaenau Ffestiniog**, then descend into darkness.

We nearly forgot: climb (or take the rack-and-pinion railway to) mighty **Mt Snowdon**!

'Take our favourite lunchtime walk from Halen Môn to the derelict Foel Ferry jetty – mountains, mussels, [Caernarfon] castle – and just gaze out to sea watching the tide.'

David and Alison Lea-Wilson, founders of Halen Môn salt makers

months. And a few miles down the Anglesey coast, Halen Môn – 'salt maker to the stars' – has gained protected food status from the European Commission, joining the likes of Parma ham and Champagne.

UNMISSABLE EXPERIENCES

The present is compelling, but the past is too. Earlier this year, Blaenau Ffestiniog's Llechwedd Slate Caverns launched a new deep-mine tour that takes visitors into the Stygian depths of Snowdonia to learn about the lives of the slate workers, the 'men who roofed the world'. The caverns are North Wales' most popular attraction for a reason – and this 150m descent into the underworld aboard Britain's steepest cable railway makes for a spine-tingling storytelling experience for young and old.

TIME YOUR VISIT

Go in August for the Menai Seafood Festival, a celebration of...guess. When you've slurped down a few locally reared oysters, walk them off on one of Anglesey's six Blue Flag beaches.

• By James Kay

03

Kangaroo Island's Seal Bay is home to one of Australia's largest sea lion colonies. The animals have been protected here since the 1950s

SOUTH AUSTRALIA

Its climate may be hot, but South Australia offers the coolest mix of brilliant wine country, abundant produce festivals, stark and stunning tracts of picturesque Aussie outback and crowd-free beaches that could make even the Bahamas jealous. The *Queen Mary 2* is putting South Australia on her travel list in 2017, choosing to dock not only in its artistic capital, Adelaide, but also taking in the rustic charms of Kangaroo Island. South Australia is a delicious feast suitable to anyone's taste.

Population: 1.7 million
Capital: Adelaide
Language: English
Unit of currency: Australian dollar
How to get there: Adelaide is served by a compact, award-winning international airport. Due to South Australia's central position, travellers can also access the state by road from various directions; the Limestone Coast road from neighbouring Victoria is among the best.

TELL ME MORE...

It's not just the abundant wine country that makes SA great. The state contains some of Australia's most breathtaking landscapes and offers a gateway to the quintessential outback experience. Take in the epic vistas of the Flinders Ranges, where the ruins of pioneer homesteads host flocks of exploring emus, marvel at the ever-changing inland water catchment of Kati Thanda–Lake Eyre or have some barefoot fun sampling the Yorke Peninsula's 700km of unspoilt sandy-white beaches.

Adelaide's best dining experience, Orana, is often described as Australia's answer to Copenhagen's Noma, with a degustation menu unafraid to proffer fare such as kangaroo tendon or green ants. Too crazy for your taste

'Due to its amazing Mediterranean-style climate, South Australia's plate offers the food traveller a feast of fresh, seasonal and stunning produce. SA's food scene is a slice of Aussie culinary heaven.'
Callum Hann, chef and TV presenter

ITINERARY
Duration: Two weeks

Jet into **Adelaide** and spend a couple of days drinking in Australia's most eclectic capital city. Ensure you've left enough time to amble through the picturesque Adelaide Hills.

Ferry across to **Kangaroo Island,** where fur-seal colonies bask in the sunshine at Seal Bay and amazing geographical features such as Remarkable Rocks and Admirals Arch are awaiting the limelight on Instagram.

Cellar-door hop through the **Barossa and Clare Valleys,** making meal stops at Maggie Beer's Farm Shop in Nuriootpa and Fino at Seppeltsfield.

Take a scenic flight over **Kati Thanda–Lake Eyre** and the Ikara-Flinders Ranges national parks.

buds? Don't worry: South Australia's bounty also includes mouth-watering Coffin Bay oysters, juicy king prawns from the Spencer Gulf, a smorgasbord of cheeses and meats from Adelaide Hills towns, and fragrant honey and honey mead from Kangaroo Island.

UNMISSABLE EXPERIENCES

• South Australia's wine country is responsible for nearly half of Australia's total oenological output, so a visit to at least a couple of its 13 distinct wine-growing regions is essential. Tempt your palate with the likes of a buttery Adelaide Hills Chardonnay or the robust blackcurrant yumminess of a Coonawarra or Clare Valley Cabernet.

• An incredible selection of food and wine events is on offer all year round. Highlights include the Clare Valley's Gourmet Weekend in May, McLaren Vale's Sea and Vines in June and the Barossa Valley's Gourmet Weekend in September.

TIME YOUR VISIT

It's not known as Mad March for nothing: if you've timed your SA trip for that month you'll find an abundance of arts and sporting events taking place in Adelaide, including the Adelaide Festival, the Adelaide Fringe, WOMAdelaide (celebrating its 25th anniversary in 2017) and the Clipsal 500 motor race.

• By Chris Zeiher

SA's diverse geography and climate lets it produce a range of wines, from dry Clare Valley Rieslings to big Barossa Shirazes

© GETTY IMAGES

83

AYSÉN, CHILE

There's only one road into the Aysén region of Chilean Patagonia and if you follow its unpaved contours from start to finish you'll experience a kaleidoscopic journey where foggy fjords give way to brooding rainforests, bone-dry pampas and powder-blue lagoons. Shaped by the forces of the Patagonian Ice Field – Earth's third-largest freshwater reserve – Aysén is an extreme landscape in constant flux. But with fresh routes to glaciers, a booming craft-beer scene in remote hamlets and a massive new nature reserve green-lit for national-park status, Patagonia's last frontier has never been such a delight to explore.

CHARLES BROOKS / CHARLESBROOKS / 500PX © CHARLES BROOKS / 500PX

Surrounded by mountains often covered in snow all year long, regional capital Coyhaique has been dubbed 'the city of eternal snow'

06

ALBERTO LOYO ©SHUTTERSTOCK

Patagonian glaciers not only look good, they taste good too: it's said their pure, cool water is what makes the local beers so refreshing

Population: 108,328
Main town: Coyhaique
Language: Spanish
Unit of currency: Chilean peso
How to get there: The small airport in Balmaceda (near Coyhaique) receives several daily flights from Santiago. Alternatively, many visitors fly into Puerto Montt and head to Aysén along the scenic Carretera Austral (Southern Hwy).

TELL ME MORE...

This is a fantastic year to experience the legacy of Doug Tompkins. Though best known as the founder of The North Face and Esprit, the American multimillionaire left the corporate

'Working on the Calluqueo Glacier is like caring for a kid, except instead of watching my kid grow, I'm watching it shrink. It's a beautiful process, but also terribly frightening.'
Jimmy Valdés, owner of Lord Patagonia Outdoors

world behind and spent his final two decades in northern Patagonia, where he purchased large swathes of land in the name of conservation. Tompkins died in his beloved Aysén in December 2015 following a kayaking accident, and his widow, Kris, is in talks with the Chilean government to donate two of their reserves

ITINERARY
Duration: Two weeks

Unwind in one of three fjord-side hot springs at **Termas de Puyuhuapi.**

Indulge in local salmon and *cerveza artesanal* at **Coyhaique's** Restaurant Dalí.

Get up close and personal with the **San Rafael Glacier** on a day trip from Puerto Río Tranquilo.

Search for guanacos and flamingos on a trek through the future **Patagonia National Park.**

Explore the fairy-tale rainforests and labyrinthine boardwalks of **Caleta Tortel.**

(Patagonia Park and Pumalín) to be used as national parks within the year. Patagonia Park, in particular, has prepared for a rush of visitors by expanding its lodge, opening a second campground, and unveiling the 23km Furioso Trail, which includes four hanging bridges over the raging Chacabuco River. A wildlife-reintroduction project has made this park *the* place to spot endangered huemul deer, grazing guanacos or even an elusive puma.

UNMISSABLE EXPERIENCES

• The San Rafael and Calluqueo Glaciers are more accessible than ever before thanks to new routes developed by tour operators in Puerto Río Tranquilo and Cochrane, respectively. Visit these cities of blue ice before it's too late.

• Patagonia boasts a burgeoning craft-beer scene that's captivated hopheads across the globe. Pure glacier water is said to give Aysén ales their crisp flavour, and 17 breweries now call the region home.

• The region's crystalline waters have also caught the attention of outdoor enthusiasts, with waterways like the Río Baker exploding into a hub for fly fishing and whitewater rafting.

TIME YOUR VISIT

Peak season in Aysén is December to March, when it's warm enough to camp, kayak and (for the brave) swim in a fjord. Book ferries and accommodation in advance during these months. Serenity seekers may consider a trip in the more temperate shoulder seasons.

• By Mark Johanson

A world of colour just offshore: threadfin butterfly fish near Fakarava Island

07

THE TUAMOTUS, FRENCH POLYNESIA

Close your eyes, and imagine this: you land on a strip of coral, surrounding a glinting lagoon of every hue from lapis lazuli to turquoise – a perfect ring of islets edged with sandbars and ruffled coconut trees. Remember that tropical paradise that appears in countless adverts? Here's the real thing. As if that weren't enough, the Tuamotus are billed as ranking among the world's best dive destinations, and that reputation has never been so justified: the number of dive areas is growing, and a new live-aboard dive boat is launching in 2017.

Population: 15,800

Main town: Rangiroa

Languages: Tahitian, French

Unit of currency: Pacific franc

How to get there: Flying is the easiest and fastest way to get to the Tuamotus. Most of the traffic is to and from Pape'ete (Tahiti). Within the archipelago, Rangiroa is the major hub.

TELL ME MORE...

The 77 or so atolls that make up this stunning archipelago are flung over an immense stretch of the Pacific. Although they're no longer a secret, the Tuamotus have managed to hold on to that slow-down-it's-the-South-Pacific feeling, and that's why they're gaining in popularity. There are no tacky resorts, just a smattering of family-run guesthouses and a couple of luxury hotels. Below the turquoise waters, a vast living world beckons divers of all levels. With its legendary drift dives, the atoll of Rangiroa has reached cult status. A 40-minute plane hop from Rangiroa, Fakarava is another iconic atoll, with heavenly white-and-pink sand, an unbelievable palette of lagoon blues and two gigantic passes that are home to an array of marine life. Those looking for an escape could opt for lesser-known beauties such as Tikehau, Mataiva or Ahe, where diving is also available.

'Diving in the Tuamotus is like visiting an underwater safari park. Sightings of big species, such as sharks, manta rays, barracudas and dolphins, are almost guaranteed every dive.'
Marco Delecluse, dive instructor on Rangiroa

ITINERARY
Duration: Twelve days

Start your adventures on delightful **Tikehau**, blessed with superb coral beaches, a supremely relaxed atmosphere and a fantastic snorkelling spot where sightings of manta rays are guaranteed.

Then head to **Rangiroa**, the stuff of diving legend, with a smattering of charismatic sites in the Tiputa Pass.

With only two guesthouses and limited infrastructure, **Mataiva** is a morsel of paradise; use your time here to come down a few gears.

Finish by visiting one of the largest and most beautiful atolls in French Polynesia, **Fakarava**, offering outstanding diving, dreamy white-and-pink coral sands and quaint accommodation options.

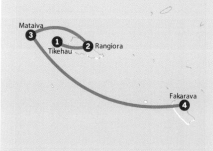

Tuamotus means 'the distant islands' or 'islands on the ocean's back'. Either way, it's the perfect place to play Robinson Crusoe

UNMISSABLE EXPERIENCES

• Tumakohua Pass (also called Southern Pass), south of Fakarava atoll, has received lots of media coverage over the last few years because of its fabulous array of fish life, especially its concentration of grey sharks at incoming tide. Go nose to nose with them on a dive.

• Rangiroa's Île aux Récifs, accessible on a boat tour, is a place like no other in the Tuamotus, with a field of raised coral outcrops chiselled by erosion into petrified silhouettes.

• The waters that lap the shores southeast of Tikehau are insanely turquoise. Swim or snorkel along the atoll's pink-and-white beaches.

TIME YOUR VISIT

The shoulder seasons (April to May and October to November) are the best times to visit. There are optimal diving conditions throughout the year, except from June to August, when the trade winds blow, producing choppy seas. Visit November to February for your best chance to see hammerhead sharks in Rangiroa.

• By Jean-Bernard Carillet

COASTAL GEORGIA, USA

You've probably heard of Savannah – you know, that southern belle with a vibrant restaurant scene and gorgeous 19th-century mansions framed by oaks dripping with Spanish moss. But most visitors never know what lies just beyond: a coastline complete with quirky towns, historic treasures and wilderness-covered islands. Wait, Georgia has a coastline? Indeed, and quite a lovely one at that. So lovely that Hollywood has taken notice and started filming major movies here, including the *Baywatch* reboot, set to release in summer 2017. So if you're seeking a coastal getaway of uncommon beauty, with plenty of adventure and without the crowds, go now, before the secret gets out.

Cumberland Island off the coast of Georgia has a fabulously photogenic beach full of driftwood

08

Population: 750,000
Main town: Savannah
Language: English
Unit of currency: US dollar
How to get there: Savannah/Hilton Head International Airport has year-round services to major American hubs, including New York, Chicago and Houston. Atlanta, which has direct international flights – as well as daily connections to Savannah – is about a four-hour drive away.

TELL ME MORE...

Travelling here isn't about ticking off the sights – it's all about the journey. This is one of America's great, unsung road trips, with surprises waiting around every bend as the lush landscape unfolds. A day might consist of long walks along driftwood-covered beaches or kicking back after a meal of fresh crabs in an open-air eatery to watch the sky light up in shades of gold and auburn at sunset. It's travelling by ferry to a forest-covered island little changed over the centuries, or stumbling upon a roadside farm stand and spooning into

'If you head down to Brunswick, try to time your visit with the first Friday of the month, when there's live music, art openings and free wine and snacks. It's always a fun time!'
Lindsey Fox, Savannah resident

Savannah, established in 1733 on the river of the same name, today boasts a thriving port and industry alongside historic charm

NATALIA BRATSLAVSKY © GETTY IMAGES/ISTOCKPHOTO

ITINERARY
Duration: Five days

Start in historic **Savannah**: visit the picturesque Wormsloe Plantation, stroll the riverfront and Forsyth Park, and enjoy southern comfort fare at Mrs Wilkes Dining Room.

Though it's the most developed of Georgia's islands, **St Simons Island** offers tracts of wilderness in its northern half. Spend some time frolicking on lovely East Beach.

Hire a bike and explore the beaches, forests and historic buildings of **Jekyll Island**. Say hello to the Georgia Sea Turtle Center's much-loved residents.

Cumberland Island offers wildlife and pristine beaches. Stay the night if you can (the Greyfield Inn is a great – and the only! – option).

the most delicious homemade peach and blueberry ice cream you've ever tasted. It's chatting with locals on porch swings who are tickled pink that you would pay a visit to their hometown. Then, of course, there's Savannah, a great bookend to your trip, where you can wander through antebellum mansions, shop in indie boutiques and eat yourself silly.

UNMISSABLE EXPERIENCES

- It's clear why the family of 19th-century industrialist and philanthropist Andrew Carnegie set up a retreat on Cumberland Island years ago: welcome to a slice of unspoilt paradise, with a mix of beaches, forests, marshes, mudflats and tidal creeks.
- Only 20 minutes' drive from Savannah, Tybee Island offers beautiful beaches and historic attractions, including Georgia's oldest lighthouse and two pre-Civil War era forts.
- Jekyll Island, once a private retreat for the likes of the Vanderbilts and Rockefellers, is a gorgeous tract of land with pristine wilderness, historic buildings and lots of outdoor activities.

TIME YOUR VISIT

There's really no bad time to visit, though summer can be incredibly humid. Springtime (March to May) is perhaps the loveliest season, when the azaleas are in bloom, and the weather is mild. Several big music festivals also happen in spring – Savannah Stopover and the Savannah Music Festival, both in March.

- By Regis St Louis

Wormsloe Plantation, a large estate created by one of Georgia's colonial founders, is today a museum dedicated to colonial life

The Ubudiah Mosque in Kuala Kangsar. Begun in 1913, construction was delayed when two elephants damaged imported marble

09

PERAK, MALAYSIA

Perak's capital, Ipoh, is nurturing a bloom of vintage-style cafes and boutiques. The nucleus of this old-meets-new makeover is Kong Heng Block, surrounding the imaginative Sekeping Kong Heng hotel. Here, cheerful joints like Roquette Cafe, Burps & Giggles and Bits & Bobs pull a vibrant crowd to shop, dawdle and slurp *ais kepal* (ice balls) in this historic neighbourhood.

Meanwhile, guesthouse owners and tour guides on Pangkor Island are starting to lead sustainable nature walks and village tours, thanks to a mentoring scheme by NGO ECOMY. In this sunbather's paradise, an emerging focus on wildlife is a breath of fresh, sea air.

FIERBAKH © GETTY IMAGES\ISTOCKPHOTO

Population: 2.5 million
Main town: Ipoh
Language: Bahasa Malaysia
Unit of currency: Malaysian ringgit
How to get there: Ipoh's Sultan Azlan Shah Airport serves Johor Bahru and Singapore, but most travellers zip up to Perak by regular, reliable buses from Kuala Lumpur to Terminal Amanjaya, 8km north of Ipoh.

TELL ME MORE...

Move over, Penang: Malaysian foodies are developing a taste for Ipoh's button-popping banquet of Malay, Chinese and Indian dishes. Locals and visitors alike guzzle *ayam tauge*, the town's signature dish of chicken and beansprouts, washed down with buttery *kopi putih* (white coffee), an Ipoh original that has spawned countless imitations across Malaysia.

Beyond Ipoh's colonial architecture and fragrant coffee steam, Perak's landscape billows with hills and limestone cliffs. This countryside once drew monks seeking solitude; these days it's rafting enthusiasts and birdwatchers who roam the wilderness, especially around lush Gopeng.
North of this tapestry of hills, rivers and limestone cliffs, rainforested Royal Belum State Park steams away. This 117,500-hectare haven for sun bears, tapirs and clacking hornbills was partially dam-flooded during the 1970s, so visitors arrive by longboat. In this primeval forest, where orchids peep above tree roots and rafflesia squat in the gloom, exploration by boat amplifies the *Heart of Darkness* vibe.

ITINERARY
Duration: Ten days

● In **Ipoh's old town**, ponder graceful colonial constructions like the Birch Memorial Clock Tower and the Moorish-style train station (nicknamed the 'Taj Mahal').

● Tour Perak's most dazzling town, **Kuala Kangsar**, home to gold-domed Masjid Ubudiah; canary-yellow Istana Kenangan, woven from bamboo; and the lavish art-deco Istana Iskandariah, the sultan of Perak's official residence.

● Refresh yourself at the verdant **Taman Tasik lake gardens** in Malaysia's 'rain city', Taiping.

● On **Pangkor Island**, enjoy resort touches such as hammocks lashed to palm trees and beachside pineapple smoothies, as well as nature walks with an ECOMY mentee.

Taman Tasik, Taiping
3
2 Kuala Kangsar
1 Ipoh's Old Town
Pulau Pangkor **4**

UNMISSABLE EXPERIENCES

Ipoh's signature dish, *ayam tauge* (chicken and beansprouts), reigns supreme in Ipoh. Locals adore Restaurant Lou Wong for its smooth chicken served with a mound of bean sprouts, seasoned just so with pepper, sesame and soy sauce.

• During the 19th century, Perak's lonely limestone crags became retreats for hermit monks. Several grew into temple complexes, like lofty Perak Tong and Sam Poh Tong, with its majestic reclining Buddha and teeming turtle pond.

• A spectacular unfinished mansion stands east of Batu Gajah. The colonial-era folly is said to be haunted by the ghost of Scottish planter William Kellie Smith, who commissioned it.

TIME YOUR VISIT

Hornbill season in Royal Belum State Park is between June and September (the best sightings are at dawn and dusk). Wildlife-lovers may wish to hang around into November and December, when migratory birds flutter into the park. Pangkor Island draws sun-worshippers almost year-round, though the wetter months are December to February.

• By Anita Isalska

'For the best breakfast in Ipoh, go to Sin Yoon Loong for white coffee, toast with egg, or Chinese noodles. From a stall just opposite, you can buy very good flat rice-noodle rolls.'

K Rajasegaran, tourist guide

SIMONLONG © GETTY IMAGES

Ipoh Old Town sprang up in the 1820s and grew as a result of British tin-mining companies flooding in

Taman Tasik Taiping was originally a tin-mining site before being turned into lake gardens in 1880

THE SKELLIG RING, IRELAND

A long time ago, far, far away...a small band of monks established a hidden base on a remote, wave-pounded hunk of rock rising out of the Atlantic like a giant triangle. With a setting like this, it's no wonder Skellig Michael made the new *Star Wars* location list. To get to this far-flung isle, a boat trip is necessary from the Skellig Ring, perhaps Ireland's most charismatically wild and emerald stretch of coastline. Glimpsed at the end of *The Force Awakens*, Skellig Michael will play a bigger role in this year's sequel and local businesses are gearing up for the expected visitor bump.

Driven the Skellig Ring?
Portmagee is your
jumping-off point to
get to the islands

10

Population: 5000
Main town: Portmagee (nearby)
Languages: Irish, English
Unit of currency: Euro
How to get there: Public transport is limited;
the area is best reached by hiring a car from Kerry
Airport, an hour and half's drive away. Boats
depart to the islands from the nearby villages
of Ballinskelligs and Portmagee.

TELL ME MORE...

Probably now best known for *Star Wars*, Skellig
Michael is also a Unesco World Heritage Site
thanks to the atmospheric ruins left by the
early Christians who eked out an existence here
from the 6th to 13th centuries. Just beyond
(and just visible in the swooping shots in the
Force Awakens finale) is the sister isle known
as Small Skellig, an even craggier outpost that
hosts a colony of 50,000 gannets, seabirds with
suitably otherworldly eyes and savage beaks. Two
specks in the ocean, at Europe's westerly edge,
the Skelligs are a challenge to reach. The 12km
crossing from the Irish mainland can be as rough
as navigating the *Millennium Falcon* through an
asteroid field, and is cancelled when the weather
is really inclement. Fortunately, the string of
villages from which the boats depart, known as
the Skellig Ring, offer other distractions – from
cosy pubs and Blue Flag beaches to historic ruins.

UNMISSABLE EXPERIENCES

• Some cruises circle the two islands, but nothing
beats actually landing on Skellig Michael and
climbing the 600 treacherously steep stone steps

'It's not the easiest to get to – and that's the point: the monks came to live
in isolation and they stayed despite everything the Atlantic threw at them.'
John O'Sullivan, manager, Skellig Experience

Skellig Michael: the Force is strong with this one – so too might the wind and waves be on the boat ride over

STEPHAN HOEROLD © GETTY IMAGES

10 BEST IN TRAVEL 2017

ITINERARY
Duration: Four days

Portmagee, with its rainbow houses, makes a great base from which to boat out to the Skelligs. Don't miss The Moorings gastropub, where *Star Wars* actor Mark Hamill himself pulled a pint.

Connected by bridge to Portmagee, **Valentia Island** is home to the Skellig Experience, an exhibition revealing the world of Skellig Michael's monks and the area's wildlife.

St Finian's Bay has a Blue Flag beach and the artisanal Skelligs Chocolate shop and cafe.

Just beyond is **Ballinskelligs**, a Gaeltacht (Irish-speaking) collection of villages, where medieval priory ruins (also built by Skellig monks) look broodingly out to sea.

to reach the intriguing, beehive-like chambers left by the monks. Book ahead – though boat licences have increased since 2015, the number of visitors per day is still restricted. And give yourself a few days in the area, in case stormy seas postpone the visit.

• For the PADI-certified, Ballinskelligs Boats runs scuba trips around the Skelligs, which also happen to be one of Ireland's best dive sites, with clear waters rich in jewel anemones, ballan wrasse, seals, jellyfish and diving gannets.

TIME YOUR VISIT
Boat trips around the Skelligs normally run April to October, with landings on Skellig Michael permitted mid-May to early October. Skellig Experience on Valentia Island is open March to November. Visit May to July and be rewarded by the sight of a circus of puffins. Whales and dolphins visit periodically throughout the year.

• By Gabrielle Jaffe

2 Valentia Island
1 Portmagee
3 St Finian's Bay
4 Ballinskelligs

TOP 10 CITIES

Bordeaux, France / Cape Town, South Africa / Los Angeles, CA, USA /
Mérida, Mexico / Ohrid, Macedonia / Pistoia, Italy / Seoul, South Korea /
Lisbon, Portugal / Moscow, Russia / Portland, OR, USA

01

The Place de la Bourse, completed in 1775,
holds the Palais de la Bourse and l'Hôtel des
Fermes, now the Musée National des Douanes

BORDEAUX, FRANCE

They used to call her the 'Sleeping Beauty', but – though she's hit the snooze button a few times – Bordeaux is now wide awake and ready for action. The new LGV Sud-Ouest line, due for completion in mid-2017, connects the city with Europe's high-speed train network and cuts travel time from Paris to just two hours. Its timing is perfect. The recently opened Cité du Vin continues the impressive redevelopment of the Garonne riverfront with a state-of-the-art wine-lovers' experience, and the city's gastronomic revolution keeps building on its own success. She's going to skip breakfast: all aboard for Bordeaux' *grande bouffe!*

Population: 236,000
Language: French
Unit of currency: Euro
How to get there: Bordeaux' airport is in Mérignac, 10km southeast of the city centre. Gare St-Jean, 3km from the city centre, is one of France's major rail transit points.

TELL ME MORE...

The Cité du Vin's vast, sinuous glass tower – already dubbed the 'Guggenheim of wine' – puts an architectural exclamation point on the rejuvenation of Bordeaux' riverfront. A Bordeaux-wide regeneration begun in 1995 saw half the entire city receive Unesco listing in 2007, making it the world's largest urban Unesco site.

It's not all about preserving the old. All but abandoned riverside warehouses are now swanky apartments, and sleepy areas like Chartrons, north of the centre, have been transformed by a new generation of design, clothing and food shops.

The buzz has spread to Bordeaux' restaurant scene. Formerly a fine-dining wasteland, the city got a shot in the arm with Joël Robuchon's La Grande Maison: in 2016, only 10 months after opening, it earned two Michelin stars. But it's

> **'Scrape Bordeaux' surface – the wide boulevards and elegant 18th-century facades – and you'll find hidden medieval side streets, buildings with interesting stories... and neighbourhoods with their own distinctive characters.'**
> *Tim Pike, expat, and blogger at Invisible Bordeaux*

ITINERARY
Duration: Two days

• Sample the delights of the **Marché des Capucins,** including Bordeaux wine and – because the Atlantic is just down the road – excellent seafood. Oysters and Sauvignon blanc for breakfast? *Pourquoi pas?*

• Climb the Gothic belfry of the **Cathédral St-André** for spectacular panoramas. The church's oldest sections date from 1096.

• Get lost among the graceful, grandiose streets of **Old Bordeaux** – don't miss the buzzy medieval lanes of the St-Pierre district.

• Behold the magical Monument aux Girondins – the most over-the-top fountain you're ever likely to see – in the **Esplanade des Quinconces**, the biggest square in France, covering 126,000 sq metres.

Bordeaux is a port city on the Garonne River, which means oysters are always fresh at the Marché des Capucins

in Bordeaux' *néo-bistrots* – small, affordable places with passionate young chefs at the helm – where you can really feel the city's gastronomic blood pulsing.

UNMISSABLE EXPERIENCES

• At Bar à Vin you'll find 30 Bordeaux wines by the glass and staff who know their stuff. And it's part of the École du Vin, so you can call your hours of sampling 'educational'.
• The Gironde riverfront is Bordeaux' new focal point. At its epicentre is the Miroir d'Eau, an immense reflecting pool; in summer, its picturesque, cooling mist is a magnet for the whole town.

• *Néo-bistrots* offer inventive food served in intimate spaces at very reasonable prices (especially at lunch). Try Miles or Belle Campagne to see what all the fuss is about.

TIME YOUR VISIT

Bordeaux is lovely year-round. Its southern location means mild winters, while summers are quite hot. The city can feel empty in August, as many locals head off on vacation; vineyards are generally too busy to accept visitors during harvest (September or October). The biennial Bordeaux Wine Festival happens in June.

• By Janine Eberle

This lively university town has the highest number of preserved historical buildings of any city in France aside from Paris

CAPE TOWN, SOUTH AFRICA

Cape Town's deceptively laid-back folk have been working hard to add cultural and culinary cred to the Mother City's famous natural charms, cementing its reputation as an African city with a global outlook. Local gastronomy is as impressive as Table Mountain's flat-topped mass, with historic wine estates in every direction, hip markets selling the fruits of the Cape's fertile terrain, and inventive restaurants winning global plaudits. The art and design scene will be given a boost in September by the opening of the Zeitz Museum of Contemporary Art Africa (MOCAA), the world's largest museum of contemporary African art and a post-industrial architectural marvel occupying a century-old grain silo.

02

The upmarket suburb of Llandudno, between central Cape Town and the Cape of Good Hope, has a great beach and good surf

Population: 3.9 million

Languages: Afrikaans, Xhosa, English

Unit of currency: Rand

How to get there: Cape Town International Airport receives direct flights from Europe and the Middle East, but you may get better deals and more choice transiting through Johannesburg.

'Surrounded by majestic mountains and with its central City Bowl overflowing with culture, food and colour, Cape Town has an amazing quality of life and captivates visitors at first sight.'

Liezel van Schalkwyk, concierge

TELL ME MORE...

As travel surprises go, you can't beat this cosmopolitan slice of holiday heaven in the dramatic centre of Africa's southern tip. Pointy-toothed predators and khaki-clad gun-toters are nowhere to be seen; indeed, the only wall-mounted antelope heads you'll spot will be made of beads and calling to souvenir hunters in the V&A Waterfront and the Woodstock neighbourhood. Likewise, South Africa's bushveld here gives way to an Instagram-crashing tapestry of mountains and vineyards, surf beaches and Smartie-box houses. First-

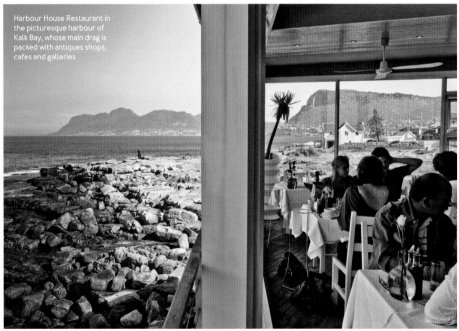

Harbour House Restaurant in the picturesque harbour of Kalk Bay, whose main drag is packed with antiques shops, cafes and galleries

GARY LATHAM © ©GARY LATHAM|LONELY PLANET

ITINERARY
Duration: One week

• Wander through the leafy Company's Garden to the **City Bowl**'s historic sights, craft markets and museums.

• Drive Chapman's Peak, one of the world's most beautiful coastal roads, to **Cape Point**, where the currents of two oceans meet.

• Learn about life in centuries past on wine estates such as **Groot Constantia**, and picnic at Buitenverwachting or Eagles' Nest.

• Cruise the design shops, galleries and cafes occupying the converted warehouses of creative **Woodstock**.

• On the **Atlantic** side, take in craft markets and the Zeitz MOCAA, followed by sundowners in chichi Camps Bay.

time visitors will be bowled over by the city's sunny sophistication and foodie creativity, with recent trends including craft beer and fynbos gin. Days mix must-sees such as Cape Point and the Castle of Good Hope with such outdoor experiences as sunset picnics on the beach and full-moon walks up Lion's Head. Community schemes offering interactive cultural tours round out your visit.

UNMISSABLE EXPERIENCES

• To reach Table Mountain's 1000m-high plateau you can ride the revolving cable car or hike up through Kirstenbosch National Botanical Garden.

• South Africa is the oldest wine region outside Europe – how could any lover of the grape stay away? As you quaff the local varietals, be sure to admire the Cape Dutch architecture on the refined estates.

• On a cultural tour you'll meet locals of all backgrounds while learning to make Cape Malay cuisine, hearing jazz in the townships and discovering the city's latest street art.

TIME YOUR VISIT

The Zeitz MOCAA is scheduled to open in September – the wildflowers will be out, but it could still be wintry. For more assuredly sunny days outside high summer, come in October, November or March. On the first and third Thursdays of every month, galleries open late and crowds wander the city centre.

• By James Bainbridge

Downtown Los Angeles
and its tallest building,
the US Bank Tower

03

LOS ANGELES, USA

Despite its reputation as a land of celebrities, health fanatics and all-around superficiality, LA has been gaining steam as a cultural destination while becoming more accessible than ever. The 2016 Metro expansion has made getting from Downtown to Santa Monica and everywhere in between much easier; city initiative Car Free LA helps tourists navigate without wheels; and almost 50 new hotels are in the works. This isn't just a beach town, either; it's a commerce capital, where movie producers and finance types mingle over sashimi and kale salads. East Coasters are moving here in droves for the sunshine and a more sustainable lifestyle.

TERENCELEEZY © GETTY IMAGES

Population: 18.4 million

Languages: English, Spanish

Unit of currency: US dollar

How to get there: The main airport is Los Angeles International (LAX), the seventh busiest in the world. LAX sits about 20 miles from downtown LA.

TELL ME MORE...

Los Angeles has more museums and theatres than any other US city, and while its big opening of 2017, the Museum of the Academy of Motion Picture Arts and Sciences (aka the Academy Museum or Oscars Museum), is likely to be pushed back to 2018, there's plenty more to explore. The Los Angeles County Museum of Art (LACMA) and the Museum of Contemporary Art (MOCA) are both major players in the art world, but there are also galleries lining nearly every neighborhood from Downtown LA to Venice. Food experiences such as the Grand Central Market and Brentwood Country Mart will keep visitors' bellies full and their curiosity satisfied – you can sample everything from Mexican to Moroccan. Discerning shoppers can find it all here, from the luxury stores on Rodeo Dr to the funky vintage boutiques on Abbot Kinney Blvd in Venice – Los Angeleno style is high-low urban-boho at its best.

'[E]veryone here is here to create and reinvent in the absence of conventional rules. In that sense it really does (still) feel like the Wild West.'

Aliza Neidich, owner of boutique Reservoir Los Angeles in Silver Lake

ITINERARY
Duration: Two days to a week

- Start in **Downtown LA**, jam-packed with everything from street art in the Arts District, to the Mexican marketplace of Olvera St, often called 'the birthplace of Los Angeles'.

- Move on to eclectic **Silver Lake**, with a large Latino population, high-end boutiques and wildly popular nosh spots, such as Intelligentsia and Sqirl.

- Then hit up **Hollywood**, taking in the TCL Chinese Theater, the Sign, the Walk of Fame and some live music at the Hollywood Bowl.

- Zip through posh neighbourhoods such as Beverly Hills and Brentwood on your way to **Santa Monica**, if only to see the infamous pier.

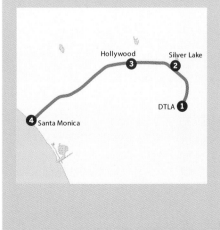

UNMISSABLE EXPERIENCES

• First-timers will want to see iconic sites such as the Hollywood Sign, the Griffith Observatory, the Hollywood Bowl and the Walt Disney Concert Hall, but they'd also enjoy exploring funky and diverse neighbourhoods such as Koreatown and Los Feliz.

• Hike through Runyon Canyon or walk around Griffith Park to get those social media–worthy snaps of the city skyline.

• Make sure to save a day for the beaches: whether you head to Venice to see the street performers or to Santa Monica pier, you'll see why the West Coast has become such a draw for so many.

TIME YOUR VISIT

Los Angeles has beautiful, temperate weather most of the year, with the (not that) wet season falling from about October to March. If you're looking to celeb spot, try January to February, when awards season is in full swing.

• By Lauren Finney

LAYLAND MASUDA © GETTY IMAGES

Venice Beach's Ocean Front Walk promenade is a carnival of fortune-tellers, performance artists and skaters

The Hollywood Sign started life as an advertisement for a local real estate development before becoming a cultural icon

04
BEST IN
TRAVEL
2017

MÉRIDA, MEXICO

Mérida's cultural offering is like no other on the Yucatán Peninsula (sorry, Cancún, you've got pretty beaches, but party culture doesn't count). On any given day you'll find a dizzying array of live music, art shows and dance performances, and the booming culinary scene is hotter than a Habanero pepper. This year Mérida has been designated the American Capital of Culture, meaning visitors can expect a ginormous cultural extravaganza as organisers stage a series of large-scale events throughout 2017. And here's the kicker: the so-called White City ranks among the safest places in Mexico nowadays.

With its huge laurel trees, shaded benches and wide sidewalk Merida's Plaz Grande has long been a focal point of the city

SAM CAMP © GETTY IMAGES/ISTOCKPHOTO

A *chacmool* at the Temple of the Warriors in Chichen Itza. These reclining figures held a bowl on their chest in which offerings were placed

MEXICO SHOOTS © GETTY IMAGES

Population: 830,732
Languages: Spanish, Maya
Unit of currency: Peso
How to get there: Most international flights to Mérida airport make connections through Mexico City. Alternatively, you can fly into nearby Cancún and catch an ADO bus from the airport terminal to Mérida's city centre.

TELL ME MORE...

Sitting regally in the northwestern corner of the Yucatán Peninsula, Mérida is a tourist town, but, simply put, it's too big to feel like a tourist trap. Sure, there are cool touristy things to do, like soaking up an evening of folkloric song and dance in Plaza Grande, but the local experience is always there for the taking – breakfast at Wayan'e, which specialises in *castacan tortas* (pork-belly sandwiches), comes to mind.

If you haven't heard, Mérida is a big-time foodie destination. Street stalls, markets and family-run eateries whip up what is arguably some of Mexico's best regional cuisine, such as *cochinita pibil* (achiote-rubbed, pit-cooked pork) and *relleno negro* (black turkey stew). An international culinary scene is flourishing too, as more and more foreign chefs take to Mérida's low-key lifestyle. And who can blame them for liking a place that makes lazing around in a hammock on a warm afternoon one of its top priorities?

ITINERARY
Duration: Three days

• Kick things off with a Yucatecan *antojito* (light snack) at a **Plaza Grande** food market.

• Then head north for a stroll along wide **Paseo de Montejo**, known for its elegant 19th-century mansions, including the iconic Regional Anthropology Museum.

• Next, rent a car to reach the Maya ruins of **Dzibilchaltún**, with a lovely *cenote* (limestone sinkhole) for swimming.

• For local flavour, continue north and spend a few nights in the laid-back port town of **Progreso**.

• The following day, head to **Santa Clara**, a small beach town where time stands still. Escapists will love the secluded Hotel Kame House.

04
BEST ⓘN
TRAVEL
2ο17

> '*A Maya market vendor best captured the essence of Mérida. I was always in a hurry and she told me, "Being in a hurry is not elegant."*'
>
> *Nelson Laprebendere, owner of Hotel MedioMundo*

UNMISSABLE EXPERIENCES

• A trip to Mérida must include a visit to the world-class Gran Museo del Mundo Maya, housing 1100 remarkably intact Maya artifacts. This is an obligatory stop for background on all things Maya before hitting the ruins.

• The secret to visiting the popular Maya site of Chichén Itzá, 120km east of Mérida, is getting there before the crowds arrive. Doing so allows you to truly appreciate some of the most astounding pre-Hispanic structures you'll ever see.

• Let loose in the fan-cooled, downtown La Negrita cantina, where live tropical tunes and mezcal drinks will have you giddily dancing into the night.

TIME YOUR VISIT

Mérida's only drawback is its sweltering heat, unless you like steamy hot weather. Avoid visiting from April to June, when the average temperature hovers around 35°C (95°F). Cooler climes prevail in January, and that's when the city hosts the month-long Mérida Fest, with fun music, art and dance events.

• By John Hecht

05

The Orthodox church of Sveti Jovan (Saint John) at Kaneo, overlooking Lake Ohrid

OHRID, MACEDONIA

■■■■ **Overlooking** the extraordinarily blue waters of its eponymous lake, Ohrid enjoys a stunning position that is best viewed from a boat. From the water you'll see the town's terracotta roofs broken up by centuries-old church spires (the city claims once to have had 365) and overlooked by the turreted walls of Car Samoil's Castle. Ohrid has transformed itself from Macedonia's religious centre to its busiest holiday resort, and its beaches are the best by far in this otherwise landlocked nation. However, a planned new lake-shore development will likely change this sleepy town forever, making now a great time to go.

Population: 55,000

Language: Macedonian

Unit of currency: Macedonian denar

How to get there: There are direct flights to Ohrid from a number of European cities, including London. There's no train station in the town, but there are buses connecting Ohrid to Skopje and Belgrade.

TELL ME MORE...

Outside the summer months Ohrid seems like a sleepy place and this is at the core of its charm: the cobbled streets with traditional Ottoman houses form a maze that leads up the hillside to the Gorna Porta, where the old town meets the ancient amphitheatre and the fortress. Here you'll still see elderly women dressed in black carrying groceries home from the market and hanging out washing over the ancient lanes to the strain of church bells. The famous churches that dot the old town and the areas around it are little short of miraculous survivors: the Sveta Sofia Cathedral is an 11th-century structure that includes Byzantine frescoes that can still be seen in the apse, while the Church of Sveti Jovan at Kaneo is one of the most photographed places in the Balkans, with its wonderful silhouette framed by the waters of Lake Ohrid beyond.

'Take a tour boat, have a cup of coffee in the old part of the city. Finish your day with lunch in some restaurant on the shore of Lake Ohrid. That is my perfect combination in my city!'

Nikola Cuculeski, professional tour guide

ITINERARY
Duration: Two days

• Start with the small but perfectly formed **Church of Sveti Jovan at Kaneo**. This ancient structure is Macedonia's most famous church.

• Clamber over the walls of the huge **Car Samoil's Castle** to enjoy superb lake views. Enjoy a performance at the **Hellenistic amphitheatre**, which hosted gladiator fights in Roman times, in the summer months.

• Take a half-day trip 30km outside Ohrid to visit **Sveti Naum Monastery**, a multi-domed stunner complete with peacocks, rose gardens and its own beach.

• Go paragliding over **Lake Ohrid** from the top of Mt Galičica, or dive around the remains of a Neolithic site in the lake's Bay of Bones.

DAVID FORMAN © GETTY IMAGES

Church frescoes depict traditional Orthodox icons of the Holy Family and the saints

UNMISSABLE EXPERIENCES

Ambling along the over-water wooden walkway past Lake Ohrid's cliffs takes you from the heart of the old town to the small sandy cove of Kaneo, perhaps the most idyllic place in Ohrid. Take a table at the ultra-relaxed Letna Bavča Kaneo, order a plate of fried fish and then cool off in the placid waters of the lake. The view of the Church of Sveti Jovan from here is magnificent, as are the craggy cliffs that surround you. Lounge about in your swimming costume drinking beers with the locals and you'll have had the quintessential Ohrid experience.

TIME YOUR VISIT

Ohrid enjoys a pleasant temperature year round, although it's definitely too cold to swim in the lake comfortably between October and April. The best months to visit are May, June and September, before or just after the flood of Macedonian holidaymakers pushes up prices and makes accommodation hard to come by.

• By Tom Masters

PISTOIA, ITALY

People sometimes refer to Pistoia as 'little Florence' for its concentration of art and architecture. And yet, despite its charms, this Tuscan town sees just a fraction of Florence's tourists. That's set to change in 2017, when the city will take its turn as Italy's Capital of Culture. Pistoia earned the title in recognition of its impressive cultural credentials and devotion to grass-roots ideas and local entrepreneurship. In return, the award offers the city an opportunity to showcase an alternative side to Tuscany: one that eschews grand-slam sights in favour of thriving small towns full of personality and dynamic, living culture.

FILIPPO MARIA BIANCHI © GETTY IMAGES

06

Population: 90,540

Language: Italian

Unit of currency: Euro

How to get there: Pistoia lies just off the motorway between Pisa and Florence. The nearest airports are Florence's Amerigo Vespucci Airport and Pisa's Galileo Galilei Airport. From Florence you can either take a BluBus or the mainline train (40 minutes). Trains from Pisa take 1½ to two hours.

TELL ME MORE...

Pistoia sits snugly at the foot of the Apennines on the edge of the Ombrone Pistoiese, a tributary of the Arno. Its medieval and Renaissance nucleus is surrounded by 3km of ramparts – just like Lucca – restored for 2017, complete with cycle trails and pedestrian pathways. Like Pisa, Pistoia has an octagonal baptistery that looks like a wedding cake, and like Siena its central piazza is a harmonious architectural ensemble that hosts an annual tournament, the Giostra dell'Orso (Joust of the Bear), every July. The €15-million windfall due to the city as part of the award will only enhance Pistoia's easy pleasures, funding an array of exhibits, festivals and social programs, and financing big-ticket projects such as the transformation of the historic Ospedale del Ceppo into a cultural centre and a retrospective of the work of native sculptor Marino Marini in collaboration with the Guggenheim.

Pageantry at the annual Giostra dell'Orso tournament

KEN SCICLUNA © GETTY IMAGES|AWL IMAGES RM

ITINERARY
Duration: Two days

● Start in **Piazza del Duomo**, one of the most beautiful town centres in Tuscany. Here you can explore the cathedral and the baptistery, and climb up the cathedral's campanile.

● Then walk a block to the **Ospedale del Ceppo**, with a famous frieze by della Robbia. It will house a cultural centre sometime this year, but beforehand you can wander its underground passages and anatomy theatre.

● Head north to the airy halls of **Palazzo Fabroni** for a blast of contemporary art.

● Then turn back south to **Palazzo del Tau** and its exceptional collection of work by homegrown talent Marino Marini.

'Pistoia has a nonchalant way of moving to a rhythm all its own. From art and culture to activism, there is an intellectual intensity here that attracts and involves all generations.'

Molly McIlwrath, art-historical tour guide at LetterArteMente

UNMISSABLE EXPERIENCES

● The beating heart of Pistoia is Piazza della Sala, a market square since medieval times. During the day, 13th-century stalls still teeter with market produce; come evening, the piazza transforms into an outdoor lounge bar.

● Climb Pistoia's sky-high campanile for awesome views over a sea of terracotta rooftops, the surrounding mountains and even Brunelleschi's famous Florentine dome in the distance.

● Alongside Florence and Prato, Pistoia is a member of the SMAC (Metropolitan System for Contemporary Art). As a result, the city is a hub for contemporary art, hosting riveting temporary exhibitions in Palazzo Fabroni.

TIME YOUR VISIT

World-renowned thinkers will descend on Pistoia for the world's only anthropology festival in May. Otherwise, July is a good time to visit due to the alfresco Blues Festival. For food lovers, autumn trumps the lot, with market stalls full of freshly harvested fare.

● By Paula Hardy

Palazzo Fabroni
❸
Ospedale del Ceppo
❷
❶
Piazza del Duomo
❹ Palazzo del Tau

The Myeongdong shopping district also offers culture in the form of Myeongdong Cathedral and the Myeongdong Nanta Theatre

SEOUL, SOUTH KOREA

For over a decade the Korean capital has been striving to become a greener, more attractive and user-friendly metropolis. Following on from successful projects such as the Cheonggyecheon, where an aging elevated highway was torn down and replaced with a central park and waterway, the city will unveil in the latter part of 2017 the Seoul Skygarden. This time, the old highway in question – a 938m-long, 17m-tall overpass next to transport hub Seoul Station – will become the platform on which trees, shrubs and flowers will be planted to create an arboretum of local species.

Population: 10 million	
Language: Korean	
Unit of currency: Won	

How to get there: Most international flights arrive at Incheon International Airport, 52km west of central Seoul; a handful land at Gimpo International Airport, 18km west of the centre. Ferries to Incheon, west of Seoul, connect the country with China.

TELL ME MORE...

Seoul Skygarden's design also includes tea cafes, florists, street markets, a library and greenhouses. Sure to be one of the most photogenic spots in an already highly Instragram-friendly city, the park will have free wi-fi – as will all public spaces in the city (including buses and subways) under Mayor Park Won-soon's Seoul Digital Plan. So snap away and post instantly to your chosen social network!

In the background you may also see Seoul's four guardian mountains: Bugaksan, Naksan, Namsan and Inwangsan. Connecting the peaks is Seoul City Wall, an 18.6km rampart first built in 1396. Over time parts of the wall were

'You can get amazing photographs of Gyeongbokgung from the roof garden of the National Museum of Korean Contemporary History.'
Robert Koehler, writer, photographer and editor of the monthly magazine Seoul

ITINERARY
Duration: Two days

• Watch the changing of the guard outside Seoul's main palace, **Gyeongbokgung**, before heading inside to tour the grand buildings, grounds and various museums.

• Next, visit the popular shopping district of **Insadong** to discover craft shops, galleries and charming teahouses.

• Survey centuries of Korean history and art at the enormous and well-designed **National Museum of Korea**.

• Near the party district of Itaewon, be amazed by the contemporary art and architecture of the **Leeum Samsung Museum of Art**.

• Finally, get a bird's-eye view of the city from **N Seoul Tower**, which sits atop the central peak of Namsan.

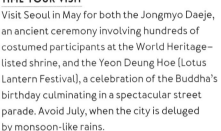

demolished, but recently the city has been restoring missing sections: around 70% (12.8km) is in place and it's relatively easy to follow a hiking route beside and, in several cases, atop the walls. Seoul's hope is that the wall will be designated a World Heritage Site in 2017.

UNMISSABLE EXPERIENCES

• Wander around Bukchon Hanok Village, a quarter of traditional one-storey wooden buildings squished between two of the city's historic palaces and rising up the slopes of Bugaksan. Some have been renovated into cafes, galleries and guesthouses.

• Join a tour at Changdeokgung palace for access to the Huwon, a 'secret garden' that's a royal horticultural idyll.

• Dining at night on delicious Korean street food at lively Gwangjang Market; the speciality is *bindaetteok* (plate-sized crispy pancakes of crushed mung beans and veggies fried on a skillet).

TIME YOUR VISIT

Visit Seoul in May for both the Jongmyo Daeje, an ancient ceremony involving hundreds of costumed participants at the World Heritage–listed shrine, and the Yeon Deung Hoe (Lotus Lantern Festival), a celebration of the Buddha's birthday culminating in a spectacular street parade. Avoid July, when the city is deluged by monsoon-like rains.

• By Simon Richmond

Gwangjang Market, a traditional street market in Jongno-gu, is home to some 200 stalls

In Seoul you'll find Buddhist temples, hyper-modern skyscrapers, over 10 million people and some of the finest local food on Earth

LISBON, PORTUGAL

It's got sights, culture and cuisine, yet Lisbon's rarely mentioned alongside southern European heavyweights such as Barcelona or Rome. If this mystifying lack of recognition is what helps the Portuguese capital remain a bargain, long may it continue. Add the weakness of the euro, and the city looks like an unbeatable deal. Should you need more persuasion, though, consider the museums: from Egyptian artefacts at Museu Calouste Gulbenkian to pop art at Museu Colecção Berardo, Lisbon groans with them, but the appetite appears unsated: a museum devoted to the history of Judaism in Portugal is coming to the Alfama district in 2017.

Designer sho
and elegant c
line Rua Garr
in Lisbon's ch
Chiado distric

RENAUD VISAGE © GETTY IMAGES

Lisbon's old town, a maze of gently winding, walkable streets that leads up to the Castelo de São Jorge

SEAN PAVONE © ©SEAN PAVONE/GETTY IMAGES/ISTOCKPHOTO

Population: 3.5 million

Language: Portuguese, but English widely spoken

Unit of currency: Euro

How to get there: Most international visitors arrive at Lisbon Airport, which lies on a spur of the city's cheap and efficient metro. Long-distance train and bus routes connect Lisbon to the rest of Europe.

TELL ME MORE...

When it comes to good looks, few cities can hold a candle to this supermodel draped over seven shapely hills on the banks of the Rio Tejo. But it's not just the angels in the baroque architecture, the clanking romance of the Remodelado trams or the by turns post-industrial and bordello-chic mood of Lisbon's many clubs – no, there's something else. Something about the painterly way in which light gleams on the polished cobbles

'From Cais do Sodré take the ferry to Cacilhas, where you can enjoy the best sunset in Lisbon.'

José Antunes, lifelong lisboeta *and expert guide from Lisbon Walker tours*

ITINERARY
Duration: A long weekend

● Thread through Alfama on your way up to **Castelo de São Jorge**, boasting panoramic views of Lisbon's roofscape.

● Hop tram E28 from Graça for a crosstown ride from **Sé Cathedral** to the white-domed **Basilica da Estrela**.

● Amble back through cafe-edged squares and mansion-lined avenues for a late-afternoon browse in the boutiques of **Chiado** and the time-warp shops of **Baixa**.

● Head up the hill for a caipirinha-powered charge around the hole-in-the-wall bars of **Bairro Alto**.

● Clear your head with coffee the next day in elegant **Principe Real**, followed by a stroll through cool **Jardim Botânico**.

of Alfama or glints on the *azulejo*-fronted facades of Lapa – something about those sun-washed or lamplit streets – makes you feel that you'll uncover an unsuspected and unforgettable travel experience here.

From the futuristic Oceanário in Parque das Nações to the Age of Discovery–era Torre de Belém, Lisbon contains enough sights to satisfy the most demanding visitor. But an aimless stroll through its streets is often as rewarding as ticking off this parade of showstoppers.

UNMISSABLE EXPERIENCES
The Miradouro de Santa Catarina is one of the best places from which to admire Lisbon's curvaceous beauty. Reach it via the Elevador da Bica funicular, which has inched up steep Rua da Bica de Duarte Belo since the late 19th century. Gaze out across the Rio Tejo to little-visited Cacilhas, where the Cristo Rei (Christ the King) statue stands with arms outspread, in the company of loved-up locals, and travellers, most of whom will never want to leave.

TIME YOUR VISIT
June is peak festival season in Lisbon. Events happen throughout the summer, but the excitement spikes on 12 and 13 June, when tens of thousands of people take to the streets to grill sardines and drink sangria in honour of Santo Antonio, the city's patron saint.

• By James Kay

Saint Basil's Cathedral was built by Ivan the Terrible to commemorate victory in war. Fittingly, it's shaped like a bonfire of flames

09

MOSCOW, RUSSIA

Russia may not have revealed all its Revolution-centennial plans, but it's as clear as a crenellated Kremlin façade that there will be radical changes in Moscow. The city will host football matches in the 2017 Confederations Cup and the 2018 FIFA World Cup, so the race is on to bring an inkling of the ultra-modern to a metropolis renowned for bombastic architecture. The new Ramenskoye Airport and a new metro line will mean an all-time high in the city's connectivity, and Moscow will gain a blockbuster attraction in the Polytechnic Museum and Educational Centre, relocated to a dramatic building in the Vorobyovy Gory hills.

Population: 12.4 million

Language: Russian

Unit of currency: Rouble

How to get there: Moscow has four international airports: Sheremetyovo (29km northwest), Domodedovo (42km south), Vnukovo (28km southwest) and Ramenskoye (43km southeast). All are connected to the centre by taxi and Aeroexpress non-stop train.

TELL ME MORE...

This year might be big, but for some time Moscow has been showing the world it's got far more in store for visitors than its iconic, dome-studded Red Sq skyline.

Besides classic culture-vulture haunts like the Pushkin Museum of Fine Art, the long list of world-class museums and galleries here is embellished on an almost annual basis. Take the Garage Museum of Contemporary Art, one of the city's foremost modern-art museums, founded by Roman Abramovich's wife Dasha Zhukova and moved in 2015 to a new location in Gorky Park, or the brand-new Russian Impressionist Museum, a mammoth collection of 19th-century Russian art in a former confectionery factory.

Moscow has really embraced the trend of converting industrial spaces into contemporary

'What I really love in Moscow is the variety, particularly with places to eat...Near the planetarium we have the café Cook'kareku ('cock-a-doodle-doo' in English): they do 24-hour breakfasts.'

Kasenia Kurilova, marketing manager

ITINERARY
Duration: Two days

• Spend your first day in the city's historic heart, Red Sq, a smorgasbord of arresting architecture. The leader of the Bolshevik Revolution rests in the square's austerely impressive **Lenin's Mausoleum.**

• Continue your Red Sq tour at domed mega-complex the **Kremlin**, comprising three cathedrals and an armoury housing the Russian state regalia. It's been the hot seat of Russian politics for centuries.

• Join Moscow's hip crowd in **Gorky Park**, where leisure activities range from boat paddling and riverside skating to table tennis and tango lessons.

• Browse the galleries at the former **Red October Chocolate Factory**, the city's hottest venue for art and nightlife. Sip cocktails enjoying sunset rooftop views of Moscow.

High spirits and nifty footwork on the Patriarchal Bridge, the Cathedral of Christ the Saviour in the background

09

BEST IN TRAVEL 2o17

art venues. Red October, Winzawod, Flakon and ArtPlay are among the former factories taken over by artists and designers, with cool cafes and clubs.

UNMISSABLE EXPERIENCES

• Russia's most splendid night out awaits at the Bolshoi Theatre, a lavish 18th-century hub of ballet and opera. Works by Tchaikovsky and Rachmaninoff have premiered here.
• Moscow's revamped green spaces, Gorky Park and Hermitage Gardens, are now vibrant centres of urban life, with music festivals, art exhibitions, street food, dance classes and public bike paths.

• You can relive decadent Tsarist Russia at Café Pushkin, one of Moscow's best restaurants, boasting a legendary vodka selection.

TIME YOUR VISIT

Summer is always an upbeat time to stop by – once the drippy spring weather is well and truly gone. Between mid-June and the beginning of July Moscow will host the Confederations Cup, when an international crowd will create a special buzz.

• By Luke Waterson

Thought there was only
one? This mock Kremlin in
Izmaylovo is a historical
theme park, though design-
wise it's more fairy-tale castle

PORTLAND, OREGON, USA

Portland doesn't try to impress anyone and so impresses everyone. It's America's city of the future: a friendly, sustainable, ethical place that values good living and leisure over acquisitiveness and ambition. Bisected by the Willamette River and surrounded by peaks, it is also a preternaturally attractive place. What better spot could there be for viewing one of nature's great spectacles: the solar eclipse of 21 August 2017. Although the eclipse will be partial in Portland, drive a few miles south into the Willamette Valley or hike up Mt Hood and you'll be cast in the moon's deep umbra between 9.06am and 11.38am (PDT).

10

The city that rose at the end of the Oregon Trail is now a prosperous bastion of liberalism and counterculture lifestyles

Population: 2.35 million

Language: English

Unit of currency: US dollar

How to get there: Portland International Airport is well served by international flights and is regularly voted one of the best airports in America. Trains to Seattle, Vancouver and West Coast cities depart from the downtown Union Station. Alternatively, the city is well served by BoltBus and Greyhound coaches.

TELL ME MORE...

Portland has the sophistication of a city several times its size but also the laid-back atmosphere of a storied old town. In the 165 years since its founding, Portland has been many cities – a

'The number of brilliant creatives here is staggering. The city is a jumping-off point to countless adventures in the natural world, which fuels inspiration.'

Josh Humbert, conservation photographer

frontier settlement, a booming timber town, a bastion of counterculture and a serious pioneer of sustainability. These days it's one of America's capitals of cool, attracting 100 new residents a day, who come for its cycle-friendly centre, verdant gardens, thriving arts scene, vintage theatres and farm-to-table food

Portland has over 500 food carts operating at any one time. Most are parked in what are called 'pods'

ANTHONY PIDGEON © GETTY IMAGES/LONELY PLANET IMAGES

ITINERARY
Duration: Two days

● Start the day with coffee at **Heart Roasters**, unless it's the weekend, in which case you'll want to head to the Saturday Market by Burnside Bridge.

● The best way to experience Portland is to wander aimlessly. The **Pearl District**, packed with boutiques and galleries, is a great place to start, then head to **Tom McCall Waterfront Park**.

● West of the waterfront, **Portland Art Museum** houses one of the most important collections of Native American art in the USA.

● In the evening **Mission Studios** serves up everything from Puerto Rican garage rock to Gulf Coast soul.

Mission Studios — **5**

The Pearl District — **2**

Heart Roasters Coffee House — **1**

Tom McCall Waterfront Park — **3**

Portland Art Museum — **4**

culture. As if this embarrassment of riches weren't enough, on the city's doorstep are the winegrowing hills of the Willamette Valley, skiing on Mt Hood and biking, rafting and zip lining in the Columbia River Gorge. The world may be surprised to discover Portland's charms, but this West Coast port is used to having it all and takes it in its leisurely stride.

UNMISSABLE EXPERIENCES

● Portland is a city of gardens, most famously its International Rose Test Garden, which will celebrate its centenary in 2017.

● Craft beer is big in Portland. Ex Novo is a recent arrival, serving inspired brews like Moonstriker, a Baltic porter made with chocolate and Habanero chillies.

● Powell's City of Books in the Pearl District epitomises Portland's community spirit and stocks a million of the world's best books.

● Portland is famous for its artisan restaurants, but the real innovation is on the street in the city's multitude of food carts. Take a tour with aficionado Brett Burmeister of Food Carts Portland.

TIME YOUR VISIT

The solar eclipse will take place on 21 August in the height of summer, when Oregon's weather should be at its best. Otherwise May and June are great times to visit, for the Rose Festival and the Grand Floral Parade. Grape stomping and harvest festivals abound in fall (September to November).

● By Paula Hardy

LONELY PLANET'S

BEST OF
THE REST

Best value destinations / Family adventure destinations /
Best new openings / Best places to stay

BEST VALUE DESTINATIONS

Seeking enlightenment through wise travel spending? Wander this way, into our annual run-through of the careful budgeter's dream destinations.

1 NEPAL

Nepal is bouncing back from earthquakes and a fuel strike that made getting round the country tough. It remains a fabulous choice for budget-conscious travellers, who can access the best of its world-famous trekking routes and underrated wildlife for well south of US$50 a day. Visitor numbers are slowly recovering and the time is ripe to get back to Nepal's mighty mountains; wherever you go, you'll receive a warm welcome, as your visit brings much-needed income to communities getting back on their feet.

The monarchy was abolished in 2008, so the King of Nepal has been replaced by Mt Everest on all banknotes.

↙ 2 NAMIBIA

Namibia's dollar, pegged to the South African rand, has been depreciating in value against many currencies for a few years, making now an opportune time to experience this amazing country. And what experiences are on offer: desert-wildlife spotting in Etosha National Park, the incredible wilderness hike through Fish River Canyon and sand surfing at the mighty Sossusvlei Dunes. Avoid South African and European school-holiday times, especially late December and January, for the best-priced flights, which generally connect through Johannesburg, or look for seasonal charter flights from Frankfurt (Germany) operated by Condor. The great blue sky, contrasted with the clear starry nights that remain the longest in the memories of many visitors to Namibia, won't cost you a dime.

Tipping is officially prohibited in national parks. In safari lodges and similar establishments it's customary to tip guides and leave a further gesture to be divided among other staff.

↘ 3 PORTO, PORTUGAL

Here's a European city that still manages to fly under the radar. It hardly seems believable given Porto's stunning setting on the Rio Douro and excellent, affordable eating and accommodation – not to mention the fleet of budget airlines from around Europe and the direct flights from New York that make getting here better value than ever. Portugal's second city has a clutch of inexpensive museums, cheap vintage trams to delight the transport nerd in your party and a pebbly beach an hour's walk along the riverbank. Atmospheric wine caves offer inexpensive tours and tastings, and day trips to vineyards are easy to arrange. The city's signature sandwich, the heart-stopping *Francesinha*, will fill your stomach with steak, ham, sausage, melted cheese and a lively tomato sauce, and might be the only meal you need to eat all day. As a bonus, one is often more than enough for two. *FC Porto, one of Europe's great football names, plays at the Estádio do Dragão. Tickets are comparatively inexpensive, this being Porto. Check www.viagogo. com for resellers.*

LONELY PLANET © GETTY IMAGES/LONELY PLANET IMAGES

↗ 4 VENICE, ITALY

Value and Venice: two things that don't often go together – yet the Lagoon City is unmissable, and scores of travellers arrive every day hoping to see it without breaking the bank. Traditionally the advice was to stay in Mestre, or even Treviso, and take the train in for the day, but this didn't allow for late-night strolls or evenings checking out the city's *osterie* (bars). Now, with locals letting out rooms and apartments on Airbnb and sites like it, you can stay in Venice itself and save money at the same time. Billeted in an area of the city away from the tourist throngs and with a kitchen at your disposal, you can have some meals in, avoid transport costs in and out of the city, and make sure you're first in the queue for Venice's heavy hitters.

Save money and queuing time by pre-booking public-transport and museum passes.
veneziaunica.it

↘ 5 DEBRECEN, HUNGARY

Hiding in plain sight beyond Budapest is Debrecen, the country's second-largest city and the heart of low-cost Hungary. Now connected by Europe's budget-airline network to seven countries, the city is opening up to international visitors. Debrecen is rich in history, but more modern influences have prompted a growing modern-art scene and streets that come alive with summer festivals. What really sets Debrecen apart is its location on the edge of Hungary's *puszta* (eastern plains). The haunt of Hungarian cowboys and home to Hortobágy National Park, the region still dominates romantic visions of traditional Hungary. *This is a part of Europe where you can find a good deal and feel like an international pioneer – a vanishingly unusual combination in this part of the world. Comprehensive trip planning information and guidance can be found at gotohungary.com.*

ROBERT FESUS © GETTY IMAGES/HEMERA

↗ 6 BELIZE

Belize is often thought of as one of Central America's pricier options – but let's take a fresh look. Here you can dive or snorkel as though you're in the Caribbean and tour Mayan ruins such as Caraco, found deep in wildlife-packed jungle that could only be in Central America. And you won't face long journeys: Belize is the same size as Wales or Massachusetts. Belize's proximity to Mexico and the Caribbean has ensured a lively and exceptionally good-value street-food scene, making budget meals effortless. Yes, there are big-ticket resorts on Ambergris Caye, but head south to Placencia and Hopkins for laid-back beach culture that's still making its way onto the map.

May and June are excellent times to visit Belize, with lower rainfall than later in the season, but fewer visitors, so lower hotel rates.

↗ 7 MOROCCO

Stable, accessible and kaleidoscopic Morocco offers a low-cost, intense hit of the exotic. There simply isn't anywhere this close to (and easy to visit from) Western Europe that remains so thrillingly at odds with that continent. Marrakesh, still unmissable, has more accommodation choices than ever before, and despite the crowds retains its timeless mix of the frenetic and the friendly. Essaouira, once an add-on to a trip to Marrakesh, can now be reached by direct flights from London and Paris. The port city of Tangier is also enjoying a renaissance, with new hotels and renovations throughout the once-dilapidated old town.

A high-speed rail link is under construction between Tangier and Casablanca, which will further accelerate change on the Mediterranean coast. The first trains should run in 2018.

BEST
OF THE
REST
BEST IN
TRAVEL
2017

INIGOFOTOGRAFIA © GETTY IMAGES/ISTOCKPHOTO

8 RUSSIA

With the rouble – at the time of writing – bumping along at tempting exchange rates against other major currencies, it's not surprising that visitor numbers to Russia have been rising. Is now the perfect moment for a visit? The trick is in how you do it. A search of Moscow's top hotels is unlikely to convince you it's bargain time, but think of it this way: with the country more affordable once you arrive, this is a good time to bite off a chunk of the Trans-Siberian Railway, taking advantage of low-cost air routes to get to and from each end. It's also a great time to visit the timeless highlights of St Petersburg. Watch for fluctuations in exchange rates, but even if these flip to the disadvantage of international visitors, by 2018 the country will see a further increase in visitors – and prices – for the FIFA World Cup, giving you another reason to go now.

Skyscanner can help you find low-cost carriers into and within Russia. www.skyscanner.net.

↘ 9 BELLARINE PENINSULA, AUSTRALIA

The Bellarine Peninsula has been a destination of choice for Melburnians looking for a laid-back (read: sleepy) escape from the city for generations. But now this part of Victoria has some tasty-looking attractions to go with its timeless beaches and historic towns like Queenscliff and Portarlington. Jack Rabbit Vineyard and Flying Brick Cider Co are two of the newer destinations attracting attention, along with a rail trail for cycling, rock pooling, snorkelling and surfing. The Bellarine is a ferry ride from the internationally better-known Mornington Peninsula and a convenient place to touch down for a couple of nights before continuing on to the Great Ocean Rd.

Up to 14 ferries a day link Queenscliff with Sorrento on the Mornington Peninsula. www.searoad.com.au.

OZGUR SUJCAK SAYS THERE IS NOTHING TO SEE DOWN HERE © GETTY IMAGES

↘ 10 MICHIGAN'S UPPER PENINSULA, USA

If you're from outside the US, you may be reading this and wondering 'Where?'. You may even be wondering that if you're American but not a Midwesterner. Either way, get ready for a locally feted region with attractions to rival national treasures. Michigan's Upper Peninsula is an area of stunning natural beauty and charming, Norman Rockwell–esque towns and villages. Because it's a destination mainly for Midwesterners, prices are reasonable, crowds are comparatively few, and the feeling of the area is casual and relaxed. The region boasts historic lighthouses, hundreds of miles of beaches and lakeshore, some of the country's oldest forests, and more than 300 waterfalls, ranging from the tiddly to the spectacular. Car-free Mackinac Island is a standout visitor draw: its 10-sq-km interior is replete with quaint shops and gorgeous views. *There are over 40 lighthouses on the Upper Peninsula lakeshore. While some are open to the public, others have new lives as B&B accommodation. www.uptravel.com.*

• By Tom Hall

FAMILY ADVENTURE DESTINATIONS

Want to try something new for your next trip? Push your family out of their collective comfort zone with these ideas for an adventure you can have together.

↘ 1 ICELAND

Travel to Iceland and within one trip your family can go dog-sledding, whale watching and glacier trekking, as well as see the Northern Lights and spend plenty of time jumping in and out of thermal pools. If that isn't adventurous enough for you, how about descending into the bowels of an active volcano?

Age restrictions and seasonal variations may apply to some activities.
www.insidethevolcano.com

↗ 2 NEW ZEALAND

New Zealand's natural beauty and excellent reputation for outdoor pursuits make it a popular destination for families. Hiring a camper van is not only an economical way to explore the country but also gives you the freedom of the open road and the fun of outdoor life without having to put a tent up each night.

Don't underestimate the distances involved: choose either the North or the South Island and plan daily distances; www.newzealand.com has a good section on driving.

3 MARRAKESH, MOROCCO

The call to prayer and snake charmers plying their trade; tiny alleys to explore; shops with wares piled high; spices, tagines and fresh juices to sample – a visit to the medina in Marrakesh is an adventure for the senses. It's also a great opportunity to learn an important skill of travelling: the art of haggling.

Prepare your kids with a positive discussion about cultural differences, hygiene rules and an emergency plan if anyone gets lost.

4 SOUTH AFRICA

Seeing animals in the wild scores pretty high on the adventure meter for most people. South Africa's Kruger National Park is recommended for children due to the high likelihood of spotting animals and the relatively small distances involved in travelling round the southern part of the park. There are also family-friendly lodges with pools for when everyone needs to cool off.

Children can learn more about elephants at the museum in Letaba. Check age restrictions before you book if you'll be travelling with children under six.

5 SNOWDONIA, UK

'Bounce below' on trampolines hidden within caves, fly through the air on a giant swing and surf an inland lagoon. It's not hard to see why North Wales made our Top Destinations list for 2017. Kids will also love adventuring through history at the many castles, climbing to the top of Snowdon and resting weary legs on a narrow-gauge railway or two.

See www.surfsnowdonia.co.uk and www.zipworld.co.uk for information on the more unusual activities available.

↘ 6 WASHINGTON, DC, USA

Exploring a world-famous city is an adventure in itself. In DC you can combine learning the art of espionage (the International Spy Museum) with a dose of history (the Lincoln Memorial, plus a range of excellent museums) and lots of fun (the elevator ride to the top of the Washington Monument, paddle boating in the Tidal Basin).

Many of Washington's attractions are free, but you may have to book timed slots in advance.

7 SOUTHWESTERN AUSTRALIA

Do your kids have their heads in the clouds? Treat them to a 600m-long treetop walk in the Valley of the Giants. Or do they prefer to go underground? Check out the fascinating caves in the Margaret River region. Is wildlife their thing? Go whale watching in Geographe Bay. Beach combing? Bike riding? Tree climbing? You've guessed it...

Catch the whales from June to early December; www.margaretriver.com is a good source of information on outdoor activities.

8 JAPAN

For robot-loving, game-playing, tech-happy teens a trip to Japan is a dream come true. Add some cerebral pursuits – discover manga and anime together or visit ancient temples and shrines – and include a visit to one of the national parks or island beaches for when everyone needs to breathe out. Before you know it, you've got a trip to please even the most reluctant adventurers in your family.

Kyoto's International Manga Museum is child friendly; Tokyo's Akihabara district has games.

SHALAMOV © GETTY IMAGES

9 SRI LANKA

Between elephants and trains, ancient temples and beaches, forts and natural parks, there's plenty to keep families busy in this little part of the Indian subcontinent. Even better, Sri Lankans welcome children with open arms, so – with a little planning and an appetite for adventure – travelling here is a rewarding experience for all.

Lonely Planet's Thorn Tree forum has useful threads on specific recommendations; bring children's sunscreen, mosquito repellent and mosquito nets, as these aren't readily available.

↖ 10 MALAYSIA

Whether you go for beaches, jungle or one of the child-friendly cities, exploring Malaysia is a great way to introduce Southeast Asia to your kids. The mix of cultures allows just enough of the familiar (colonial architecture, shopping centres, Western food) for when the exotic (the heat, the flavours, the bustle) becomes overwhelming.

Nearby Singapore is a natural starting point, with some fantastic attractions for kids. Older children will enjoy spotting animals in the jungle parks.

• By Imogen Hall

BEST NEW OPENINGS

Want to be the first through the door? Discover exciting projects and attractions in the pipeline around the world for the year ahead.

1 MUSEUM OF THE AMERICAN REVOLUTION

With the inauguration of a new American president in 2017, take a deeper look at the politics and culture that shaped this nation. The Museum of the American Revolution explores this tumultuous and transformative time in American history. Filled with historic objects and artefacts, the museum will house permanent and special exhibitions, as well as multimedia experiences, including a theatre housing the actual tent that General George Washington used as his headquarters and home for most of the war.

Located in the heart of historic Philadelphia, start your trip here before exploring nearby iconic sites, including Independence Hall.

② LAVA, HVOLSVÖLLUR, ICELAND

Tectonic drama is an Icelandic speciality, whether you're talking hard-to-pronounce volcanoes, fiery Viking myths or Verne's *Journey to the Centre of the Earth*, which was set here. This state-of-the-art centre offers an earthquake simulator, artefacts and a viewing platform overlooking the volcanoes Eyjafjallajökull, Katla and Hekla. Take a tour to get closer to the action. *LAVA (lavacenter.is), in Hvolsvöllur, Southwest Iceland, opens in May 2017.*

③ KI WILDERNESS TRAIL, KANGAROO ISLAND, AUSTRALIA

The newest walk in Australia, the soon-to-be-iconic Kangaroo Island Wilderness Trail will take you around some of this South Australian island's most spectacular landscapes. On the way you'll wander through mallee forest and along clifftops, beaches and freshwater lagoons, passing abundant wildlife as well as photogenic natural formations like Remarkable Rocks and Admirals Arch. The first part of the walk – the Rocky River hike – opened last year, with the final section slated for completion in late 2016. *The KI WIlderness Trail is a 63km, 5-day walk; www.walkingsa.org.au*

④ MUSÉES YVES SAINT LAURENT PARIS AND MARRAKESH, FRANCE AND MOROCCO

Fashion designer Yves Saint Laurent is set to have not one, but two museums opened in his honour. Saint Laurent's former atelier in Paris will be refurbished to its original style, giving visitors the chance to get a sense of his workspace as it would have been. A second museum will be set near the designer's beloved Jardin Majorelle in Marrakesh. A number of his creations will be displayed here, alongside a library, cafe, and other exhibitions. *Both museums are set to open in September 2017. Visit www.fondation-pb-ysl.net/ en/Musees-YSL-Paris-826.html for more information.*

TYRHOONSKI © GETTY IMAGES/ISTOCKPHOTO

AKAGERA NATIONAL PARK, RWANDA

Rwanda has long been famous for its gorillas in the mist, which reside on the jungle-clad slopes of Volcanoes National Park, but it's another of the country's national parks that will be making headlines in 2017. Akagera is reintroducing black rhinos to its wilderness, and thus completing the return of the Big Five (lion, leopard, elephant, buffalo and rhino).

Track Africa's most iconic creatures with a local safari operator registered with the Rwanda Tours and Travel Association (www.rttarwanda.org)

AMERICAN WRITERS MUSEUM

Chronicling the American experience is a national obsession. The new American Writers Museum offers a look into how the literature of the USA has documented and influenced the culture of the nation. Located in Chicago, the mission of this museum is to engage the public with the profound ways writers have shaped the way America sees itself.

Dive deep into Chicago's literary landmarks, including Hemingway's birthplace and the stockyards immortalised in Upton Sinclair's The Jungle.

BEST OF THE REST
BEST IN TRAVEL 2017

7 CRUISE (ALL OVER THE WORLD)

Cruising the Med? Check. Cruising the Orient? Check. Cruising the South Pacific? Check. A new cruise in 2017 will have you checking yourself in around the globe, from Miami to London on a 141-day long journey. Stopping at 66 different locales, including Cuba, Bora Bora, Hong Kong, Mumbai and Malta, this remarkable sailing will be the maiden voyage of the *Viking Sun*.

Tickets for Viking Cruises (www.vikingcruises. co.uk) first-ever round-the-world cruise start at about US$45,000.

8 PINKY'S ECO RETREAT AND BEACH CLUB ON ROTTNEST ISLAND, WESTERN AUSTRALIA

A new tented eco retreat, Pinky's is set to open in 2017 on Rottnest Island, a nature reserve famous for its wildlife and beaches, and just 30 mins from Perth by ferry. The glamping retreat will include 29 luxury eco-tents with ensuites, 10 affordable two bedroom 'family' tents as well as 35 backpacker or budget tents. Its eco credentials include recycling water, using solar energy and sustainable building practices and products. Rottnest is a car-free island with 63 white sand beaches, snorkelling trails and the quokka, a photogenic marsupial similar to pint-sized kangaroo, as well as whales, dolphins and seals.

Prices start from AU$75 per night. Visit www.facebook.com/pinkysrottnestisland for more information.

9 EDEN PROJECT HOTEL, CORNWALL, UK

The Eden Project has transformed an abandoned Cornish clay pit into a hugely popular, plant-packed attraction. The landscaped site and its bubble-shaped biomes contain everything from giant corpse flowers to bananas, cacti and ivy gourd, and a treetop walkway gives a lofty perspective on the greenery. There's already a YHA hostel here, and this £6 million new hotel will offer comfort in a 115-bedroom space that – surprise surprise – is designed to 'blend into the countryside'.

The Eden Project Hotel (www.edenproject.com) opens in mid-2017.

10 DESIGN SOCIETY, SHĒNZHÈN, CHINA

In 2017 the Shékŏu area of Shēnzhèn will welcome a brand new cultural hub in collaboration with London's renowned V&A Museum. Design Society's V&A Gallery will focus on 20th and 21st century international design, with exhibits ranging from the latest drone technology to a meticulously embellished Christian Dior dress. There will be two major touring exhibitions in 2017 and 2018.

Alongside its museum, Design Society will feature a theatre and a public event programme. Follow the V&A blog for more: vam.ac.uk/shekou.

BEST PLACES TO STAY

Don't settle for any old lodgings. Here are our picks for 2017's most extraordinary places to rest your head.

↘ 1 A HOUSE FOR ESSEX, UK

Sometimes accommodation is so unique and sought-after that the only way to stay there is via ballot. That's been the case for British artist Grayson Perry and FAT Architecture's collaborative 'House for Essex'. Part artwork, part country folly, the project is designed to appear 'as a small, beautifully crafted object amongst the trees and fields' by the River Stroud. The house contains artworks – including tapestries, vases and mosaic floors – by Perry that celebrate Essex. *Ballot winners can stay with three friends. www.living-architecture.co.uk/ the-houses/a-house-for-essex/ overview*

↗ 2 TREEHOTEL, SWEDEN

In Sweden's Harads woods, the super-quirky Treehotel offers five unique luxury tree houses – the Cabin, the Mirrorcube, the Bird's Nest, the Blue Cone and the UFO – with a sixth opening early 2017. Each beautifully furnished tree house has a toilet and washbasin; a 'tree sauna', hot tub and showers are in a nearby building. *You can nordic ski in winter, and horse ride over summer. www.lonelyplanet.com/sweden/ norrbotten/hotels/treehotel*

3 Z HOTEL NY, USA

Perched by the Queensboro Bridge off 59th St, the Jazz Age—inspired boutique Z Hotel NY has astounding views of Manhattan from across the East River. The sleek 14-storey tower offers 100 snug, stylishly decorated rooms. After a day walking New York's hectic streets, this Long Island retreat's rooftop bar is the place to watch the sun set and the lights twinkle across the Manhattan skyline.

The hotel's excellent transport links include eight subway lines and the NY Water Taxi ferry. www.zhotelny.com

4 SAL SALIS, AUSTRALIA

Sleeping in wilderness tents, built on individual wooden platforms nestled among sand dunes, metres from pristine Ningaloo Reef in Western Australia, is about as quintessentially Oz as it gets. Guests swim, snorkel or kayak at Australia's 'other' dramatic reef – famous for humpback whales, whale sharks, dolphins, turtles and manta rays – and dine on bush-inspired meals 1300km north of the closest capital city, Perth.

Staffed by a young, friendly and informed team, this place defines the Australian experience. www.salsalis.com.au

↘ 5 HENN NA HOTEL, JAPAN

Whether gimmick or quest for cost efficiency, Henn na Hotel in Sasebo, southwestern Japan, is the world's first hotel to be staffed by robots. At reception are two multilingual robots; the velociraptor speaks English. Facial-recognition technology replaces the standard electronic key, and your luggage is delivered to your room by automated trolley. In the lobby, a robot arm stacks storage boxes into the locker wall.
Stay for a glimpse of the future. www.h-n-h.jp

6 SCOTLAND YARD LUXURY HOTEL, UK

The original Scotland Yard has been reimagined as a five-star luxury hotel, to be run by German hotel group Steigenberger in 2017 after a £50-million refurbishment. Housing the London Metropolitan Police Force from 1829 to 1890, Scotland Yard featured in tales by Charles Dickens as well as real-life dramas such as the Jack the Ripper investigations.
Bang to rights it'll cost you to stay here. Check www.steigenbergerhotelgroup.com/en/home.

7 MANDALAY, ST VINCENT & THE GRENADINES

On the 'fantasy island' of Mustique, the Balinese-inspired former holiday home of David Bowie is now available for short-term rentals. Five-bedroom 'Mandalay' was built in 1989 on a 2.5-hectare plot with commanding views of gorgeous Britannia Bay. The house boasts an infinity pool, dining pavilion, games room, study and, of course, music studio.
Staying here will run you a cool $40,000

per week (in low season), with a maximum of 10 guests. www.mustique-island.com/villa/mandalay/overview

8 TOBOLSK PRISON CASTLE HOSTEL, RUSSIA

Russia's notorious Tobolsk Prison Castle has become a hostel. Built between 1838 and 1858, the Siberian prison housed tsarist and Soviet exiles as well as intellectuals such as Fyodor Dostoyevsky. Learn more about their experiences by booking a stay in one of the former solitary-confinement cells, known as 'sweat boxes'. The prison was closed in 1989, and today the site includes a city archive, museum and library.

Rug up: Siberian winters are bone-chillingly cold. www.lonelyplanet.com/news/2016/01/28/siberias-prison-castle-turned-into-tourist-hostel

9 QUIRPON LIGHTHOUSE INN, CANADA

Canada's coasts are replete with beautiful lighthouses made obsolete by 21st-century technology. This 1922 lighthouse-keeper's house at the base of the still-operating Quirpon Lighthouse is now a B&B where 21st-century technology is obsolete. Things to do: boat tours to view icebergs, seabird spotting and watching migrating whales. Things you cannot do: watch television, talk on the phone or use social media. For rustic but comfortable, this is perfect.
Quirpon is stunning year-round. www.linkumtours.com/quirpon-lighthouse-inn

↖ 10 WHARE KEA LODGE & CHALET, NEW ZEALAND

Located at 1750m a short hop from Mt Aspiring National Park, this chalet has simply spectacular views. For four months a year it's snow-covered; in summer the mountainside is dotted with wildflowers. Guests can go skiing, walking, cycling, canyoning and kayaking in the area. Every two years the owners host a writer or visual artist to inspire their creative output with the Kenneth Myer Prize. Time to get creative!
Accessible only by helicopter; 20 minutes from Wanaka. A cool NZ$4600 per night.

• By Tasmin Waby

LONELY PLANET'S

TOP 5 TRAVEL TRENDS

Micro-distilleries / The world is your office /
Bikepacking / Be Instavidual / Sustainable travel

MICRO-DISTILLERIES

Over rosé? Bored by craft beer? There's no need for sippers to stress. The latest craze is to sample spirits produced with locally sourced ingredients at a regional micro-distillery. From award-winning small-batch gins in Australia to peaty single-malt whisky in northern Japan and experimental vodkas in the US, there's no denying that the craft-spirit-making zeitgeist is upon us.

BOX DISTILLERY, ÅDALEN, SWEDEN

Poking out of dense forest on the shores of the spectacular Ångermanälven River in remote northern Sweden is Box Distillery. And for this picturesque distillery it's all about the location: the crystal-clear river, where 500,000 litres of cold mountain water flows by each second, combined with the region's wide temperature variations, results in Scandinavia's most distinctive whisky.

From June to August Box Distillery is open daily for tours; it has a restaurant and bar. boxwhisky.se

INDUSTRY CITY DISTILLERY, BROOKLYN, USA

Vodka by self-proclaimed nerds! Industry City Distillery can be found in the shared space of Brooklyn's Industry City and approaches its sugar-beet-vodka crafting from a scientific angle. All equipment was built on the premises, resulting in a very experimental approach to distilling.

Fancy a cocktail with views of the bay? Friday and Saturday nights from 4pm to 10pm is cocktail time at Industry City's tasting room. drinkicd.com

YOICHI DISTILLERY, HOKKAIDO, JAPAN

Japanese whiskies currently take pride of place in some of the world's finest drinking establishments. Nikka Whisky – 2015 International Distiller of the Year – produces much of its award-winning peaty single malts at its Yoichi Distillery. Located close to Sapporo in southern Hokkaido, the handsome distillery is flanked by mountains and the Sea of Japan.

Taste up to three whisky blends on the distillery tour; self-guided tours are also available. www.nikka.com

THE BOTANIST, ISLAY, SCOTLAND

Scotland may be the home of whisky, but on the Hebridean island of Islay you'll find a micro-distillery dedicated to creating a floral gin with foraged botanicals. The all-important raw ingredients, picked from Islay's shores, hills and bogs, are distilled to create a contemporary gin.

Book the full warehouse experience for an insight into the distilling process and philosophy. www.thebotanist.com

↗ FOUR PILLARS, HEALESVILLE, AUSTRALIA

This sophisticated small distillery, spearheading the micro-distillery explosion in Australia, sits in the heart of Victorian wine country and offers a delicious alternative to the abundance of cellar doors in the surrounding Yarra Valley. Four Pillars is dedicated to crafting gin using native Australian botanicals such as lemon myrtle and Tasmanian pepperberry.

About an hour's drive from Melbourne, Four Pillars' contemporary tasting room rivals many a wine-country cellar door.
www.fourpillarsgin.com.au

SIPSMITH, LONDON, ENGLAND

Sipsmith Distillery is one of five licensed gin distilleries located in the London area and the first to be granted a local license for a copper-based still since 1820. This handcrafting specialist produces gin and vodka in small batches with reference to the English countryside. For instance, Sipsmith's delicious sloe gin has been rested on a bed of wild sloe berries, creating an extraordinary burgundy hue. It's a must taste!

Book tours in advance and take place on selected weekday evenings. www.sipsmith.com

64° REYKJAVÍK DISTILLERY, REYKJAVÍK, ICELAND

Sourcing subarctic berries to create delicious schnapps is 64° Reykjavík's speciality. Using handpicked ingredients from the wilds of Iceland, this distiller's offerings include crowberry schnapps, made from the small, juicy black berries that only grow in the subarctic tundra, and the traditional Icelandic spirit *brennivín*, a strong schnapps flavoured by caraway and angelica seeds.

The distillery isn't open to visitors, but you can try its delicious products at Iceland's best cocktail bar, Reykjavík's Slippbarinn. www.slippbarinn.is

GLENDALOUGH DISTILLERY, GLENDALOUGH, IRELAND

Ireland's first craft distillery, started by five friends, Glendalough is safeguarding Irish distilling heritage by reintroducing *poitíns* ('the water of life') to the world of spirits. Once expertly crafted by monks, *poitíns* was outlawed by King Charles in 1661, which sent it into obscurity. Glendalough now makes the spirit in three strengths: Premium Irish, Sherry Cask Finish and the ominously named Mountain Strength.

The distillery doesn't offer tastings, but poitíns can be enjoyed nearby at The Wicklow Heather, in the village of Laragh. www.wicklowheather.ie

POLI 1898, VENETO, ITALY

Not all craft distillers are new kids on the block. The family-run Poli distillery has been making fine grappa in the heart of the Veneto for more than a century. Key to its highly sought-after grappa is the sourcing and prompt distilling of quality raw materials using a combination of traditional and bain-marie stills.

Poli offers guided tours. www.poligrappa.com

HARTFIELD & CO, KENTUCKY, USA

The Kentucky Bourbon Trail, where fabulous small-batch distillers litter the bluegrass fields, is a well-worn path for most spirit enthusiasts. The first distiller since Prohibition to be granted a licence in bourbon country, Hartfield & Co prides itself on sourcing ingredients from within 10 miles of the property where possible. This is craft distilling at its finest.

The Saturday 'County Tour' includes an in-depth look at Hartfield's processes and finishes with a tasting. www.hartfieldandcompany.com

• By Chris Zeiher

THE WORLD IS YOUR OFFICE

All work and no play? Not any more. Due to online freelancing, mobile tech and co-working spaces, more and more travellers are earning on the road. For these 'digital nomads', the world is a gig and anywhere is your office.

REMOTE CONTROL

The concept of 'bleisure' (mixing business trips with pleasure) is as old as the hills, but the rise of the online 'collaborative economy' has opened up the world of working remotely to a new generation – and not just those flying business class.

Initially, these new kinds of workers, sometimes dubbed 'digital nomads', 'e-workers' or 'backhackers' (OK, we made the last one up), were mostly creative, academic or tech professionals. They were writers typing away on a beach in Thailand, graphic designers working on creative projects in an Amsterdam cafe or developers coding while, quite literally, on the fly. But more and more industries are catching on to the benefits of remote work.

Forbes says that 34% of the US workforce is now considered freelance, and this is set to rise to 40% by 2020. The economic crisis of 2008, mobile and cloud technology, and the influence of social networks like Facebook and LinkedIn have created a 'perfect storm' for the freelance age.

GREAT GIG IN THE SKY

Just 10 years ago, if someone wanted to be a freelancer they needed contacts – lots of them. Today, they just join peer-to-peer sites like Upwork, Fiverr or any other marketplace where sellers can connect directly with buyers all over the world.

Initially popular with millennials and twenty-somethings who realised they could 'gig their way around the globe', remote work is now the choice of people of all ages. Semi-retirees building second careers while overseas, gap-year students earning as they go, young families on short-term relocations – the line between work and wanderlust is blurring.

While the upsides are clear – you get to see the world without going bankrupt – there are some potential downsides: instability, cash-flow problems and 'zero-hours' contracts, to name but a few. An often-overlooked aspect is not being able to fully appreciate a place if you're too engrossed in your inbox. So it's important to manage your time on the road and allow yourself moments to stop and explore.

THE WORLD IS YOUR OFFICE

TOP
FIVE
TRENDS
BEST IN
TRAVEL
2017

THE SPACE RACE

Virtually anywhere can be a workplace today, whether it's a hotel lobby, a cafe or even a park bench. But a very clear sign of this new way of working can be seen in the rise of co-working spaces. These cater for those who enjoy the comforts of an office, with unlimited wi-fi, printing and, of course, free coffee.

These shared office spaces give freelancers the chance to discuss ideas with like-minded people and they usually offer daily, monthly or yearly passes to use a desk or room. Co-working networks such as Copass and WeWork are growing at the speed of light, with new locations springing up in cities all over the world.

Hot spots include hipster havens like New York, London, Berlin and Amsterdam, but shared workspaces are also popular in backpacker hubs. Thanks to the low cost of living, international schooling and welcoming expat communities, Ubud in Bali and Medellín

Hubud, a collaborative working space in Ubud, Bali

© FRANZ NAVARETTE FRANZNAVARRETE

Check out 10 of the best workspaces worldwide...

BETAHAUS, BERLIN, GERMANY
Co-working space and cafe.
www.betahaus.com/berlin

URBAN PLACE, TEL AVIV, ISRAEL
In the heart of the 'start-up nation', on leafy Rothschild Blvd; offers Mediterranean views. urbanplace.me

PUNSPACE, CHIANG MAI, THAILAND
Has two locations, in Nimman and Tha Phae Gate, with snacks, coffee and 24⁄7 access. www.punspace.com

LAPTOP, PARIS, FRANCE
Cosy spaces and meeting rooms set in refurbished 19th-century digs. www.lelaptop.com/en

THE FARM, NEW YORK, USA
Located in SoHo, this co-working haven even has a tree house. www.thefarmsoho.com

COWO|360, ROME, ITALY
Bright, modern and airy workspace in northeast Rome. workitout.it

KINDRED STUDIOS, MELBOURNE, AUSTRALIA
Not just a workspace but also has studios, a bar and yoga classes. www.kindredstudios.com.au

THINKING HUT, AMSTERDAM, THE NETHERLANDS
Co-working space set in a converted stable building dating from 1912. www.thethinkinghut.com

HUBUD, UBUD, BALI
Vibrant expat 'hub in Ubud' decked out in artisan bamboo, with views across rice fields. www.hubud.org

ONDAS, MEDELLIN, COLOMBIA
Cafe, co-working space and Spanish language school rolled into one. www.ondasmedellin.com/coworking

in Colombia are firm favourites with freelancers. Chiang Mai in Thailand, more known for its elaborate temples, is also growing as a centre for 'tech travellers' due to its mild climate and '*farang* (European)-friendly' services; it will host the Coworking Unconference (www.cuasia.co) in February 2017.

• By Dan Savery Raz

BIKEPACKING

Mark the bicentenary of the birth of the bike – or 'velocipede' as Karl Drais called his invention in 1817 – with these multi-day off-road cycling adventures.

↗ ALPS 2 OCEAN TRAIL, NEW ZEALAND

From the shapely ankles of New Zealand's highest mountain, mighty Aoraki (Mt Cook), the new 301km (188-mile) Alps 2 Ocean Trail cascades through the foothills of the Southern Alps, sending cyclists past great lakes and along rivers wending across the Canterbury Plains, until it reaches the Pacific Ocean at Oamaru. The final sections of this magical mixed-terrain trail are slated to open in 2017.
Allow four to six days for all nine stages. There are camping facilities along the route. www.alps2ocean.com

ICELAND

If you're armed with chunky tyres, the tortured terrain of Iceland is ideal for epic off-road sagas, with adventures aplenty to be had amid a volcanic landscape fringed by fire and snow. The elements are in charge, so keep plans loose, but an excellent loop links the Fimmvörðuháls and Laugavegur trails between Landmannalaugar's hot springs and the glacial valley of Þórsmörk, via the stunning Skógafoss waterfall.
Allow four to five days for the 85km (53-mile) circuit. There are huts and campgrounds along the route. www.volcanohuts.com

DARTMOOR & EXMOOR, UK

Southwest England's Dartmoor and Exmoor boast brilliant biking trails and beautiful bivvying spots (Dartmoor is the only part of England where wild camping is officially permitted). Link them with a multi-day meander along bridle paths and across open terrain shadowing the Two Moors Way, a long-distance trail from Lynmouth on the North Devon coast to Ivybridge.

Not all of the 160km (100-mile) Two Moors Way is rideable, but you can plot your own course. www.devon.gov.uk/walking/two_moors_way.html

↙KOKOPELLI TRAIL, USA

Linking two mountain-biking meccas, Colorado's Fruita and Utah's Moab, this 240km (150-mile) rocky route is a roller-coaster ride across the desert plateaus and mountain passes of the American West, rearing from 1200m to almost 2740m. Almost entirely off road, the terrain ranges from technical single track to sandy paths. Expect leg-crushing climbs and rubble-rousing descents.

Allow three to six days to ride the route independently, or check out the annual four-day race: www.bikerpelli.com

⭨MUNDA BIDDI TRAIL, AUSTRALIA

Meaning 'path through the forest' in the tongue of the Noongar people, the Munda Biddi Trail is an unparalleled off-road odyssey that cuts a serpentine route across 1000km (600 miles) of stunning hinterland from Mundaring on Perth's outskirts right down to Albany. Rolling through river valleys, aromatic eucalypt forest and beautiful bushland, the non-technical trail takes three weeks to cycle in its entirety but is divided into multiple standalone sections.

Avoid summer. Cycle-friendly campgrounds and huts line the route. www.mundabiddi.org.au

BILL HATCHER © GETTY IMAGES\NATIONAL GEOGRAPHIC CREATIVE

⭨CAIRNGORMS, SCOTLAND

Scotland's excellent outdoor-access code allows you to (respectfully) rough ride and wild camp anywhere, including Highland mountain passes. Complete a stunning loop of Britain's second-tallest peak, Ben Macdui, by combining the classic Cairngorm trails of Lairig Ghru and Lairig an Laoigh for a 59km (37-mile) overnight adventure. Not for the faint-hearted, this fair-weather-only route requires the odd bout of boulder-field hike-a-bike action but also offers some sublime single-track and fantastic downhill sections.

Stay in Corrour Bothy or camp.
www.walkhighlands.co.uk

MONKEY PUZZLE TRAIL, CHILE

Dirt roads and aorta-busting Andean ascents are signatures of this stunning 233km (145-mile) trail, which leaves Melipeuco and ducks below the curious and colourful umbrellas of Araucanía's monkey puzzle (araucaria) trees in Reserva China Muerta, before climbing above Chile's Lake District and traversing an alpine pass on the high flanks of Volcán Lonquimay in Reserva Nacional Malalcahuello-Nalcas. Horse trails provide off-road options through the twin reserves, or ride the rough road to Ralco.

Allow four days. www.bikepacking.com ›
Dirt Touring Araucanía

TOP
FIVE
TRENDS
BEST IN
TRAVEL
2017

DRAGON'S SPINE, SOUTH AFRICA & LESOTHO

Follow pedalling pioneers David Bristow and Steve Thomas, authors of *Riding the Dragon's Spine*, on this epic 3840km (2400-mile) rolling romp across South Africa and the highlands of Lesotho to the Zimbabwean border. The 58-stage route traces unsealed trails from Cape Town and the Western Cape vineyards, past Swaziland and through the rarefied air of the high country to the banks of the great grey-green Limpopo River.

Download free GPS tracks here:
www.dragontrax.co.za.

BASQUE COUNTRY, SPAIN

The hinterland and hills of Basque country arguably offer Europe's tastiest trails, from sublime single track hugging surf-soaked coasts to rolling rosé-hued routes through the Pre-Pyrenees. In summer, take a tarp and splice together a multi-day mission around a 450km (280-mile) loop, beginning in Bilbao, heading west along the coast and a section of the Camino del Norte to San Sebastián, before turning inland and pedalling uphill to explore Aralar, Urbasa and Gorbea national parks.

Allow eight days. www.basquemtb.com,
www.tourintune.com

BACKCOUNTRY MONGOLIA

Unsurprisingly, the land of Chinggis Khaan, famous for free-range horse-trekking adventures, also offers brilliant backcountry bikepacking. Steer your steel-framed steed across the steppe in any direction, negotiating equine-etched trails between friendly yak-and-yurt villages and pitching your tent wherever you please. In the Central Mongolian aimag of Arkhangai, a fantastic 480km (300-mile) route loops around Terkhiin Tsagaan Nuur (White Lake) in the Khangai Mountains near Tariat Sum.

Allow six days. www.bikepacking.com ›
Khangai Mountains Traverse

• By Pat Kinsella

URBANCOW © GETTY IMAGES/ISTOCKPHOTO

@ihavethisthingwithfloors *In June 2014, in a bar in Amsterdam, we discovered that all three of us had been sharing pictures of our feet on beautiful floors. That night we created an Instagram account. We added, 'When nice feet meet nice floors, make a selfeet', and our little adventure began.*

BE INSTAVIDUAL

Don't be an Instagram clone: lose the sunset cliches and explore the extraordinary – your way. Here are our picks of travel Instagrammers who show us a world unlike any other.

@paperboyo *In a bid to create something different when photographing London, I started transforming London's landmarks with a variety of cut-out paper shapes. People got on board with the amalgamation of forced perspective, humour and papercutting. Now I travel the world with my camera, scalpel knife and a big wedge of black paper.*

@serjios *'It's not what you see but how you see it' has been my motto since day one on Instagram. I try to show that it is possible to bring the ordinary closer to art by focusing on things everyone takes for granted.*

@slinkachu_official *I photograph miniature figures on the streets of cities around the world. The installations respond inventively to the environment, but also comment on the way urban areas affect us. Anonymity, loneliness, artificiality; these themes resonate in all cities. After taking the pictures, I leave the figures to be found, overlooked or destroyed.*

@dailyoverview *I aim to inspire a new perspective by showing the Earth from above like never before. Using the highest resolution satellite photographs, I offer a new way to look at the landscape that we have shaped and the vastness that surrounds us.*

@lee_jeffries *My photographs are the final piece of a long, emotional journey. I venture out onto the street simply to be with people. I often say, in a strange kind of way, I fall in love with the people I meet. The photographs I take are the act of saying goodbye.*

@CrisGravin *My theme is architecture, with a special focus on staircases. Staircases captivate me; they reveal a new dimension when viewed top down or bottom up. I take great care in alignment when choosing my point of view, so that no detail is lost in my final composition.*

@beau_johnston_photography *You have to be willing to take a beating to photograph waves. The longer you hang in there, the greater the risk, but also, the greater the reward. It's worth it when you're out there! The textures, colours and power of the ocean are what captivate me to share its natural beauty.*

@daniel__lau *When you see a city from such a height, everything slows down. It's like the city is in slow motion. You don't hear anything and you don't feel the pressure. It's a state of meditation.*

@andrewknapp *I never travel without my sidekick, a border collie named Momo. For me, it's all about the things we discover by accident, and how traveling with a dog connects us in a different way with our environments. We'll take the back roads as much as we can, and it'll usually lead us to some unpredictable, incredible things.*

SUSTAINABLE TRAVEL

The International Year of Sustainable Tourism for Development is the perfect time to start thinking about how you can make travel decisions that benefit the planet and its peoples, as well as yourself.

↗ BEARS IN ALASKA

With one transatlantic flight adding as much to your carbon footprint as a year's worth of driving, look for travel opportunities in your own backyard. The 355 million residents of the US and Canada might consider Alaska, with its endless low-impact adventures. Viewing its three species of American bear – especially the polar bear, whose environment is increasingly threatened – is as educational as it is awe inspiring.
Look for operators with Adventure Green Alaska (www.adventuregreenalaska.org) sustainable-tourism certification.

WHALES & DOLPHINS IN THE AZORES

Witnessing whales and dolphins breaching and frolicking in their natural habitat is arguably one of the world's most thrilling wildlife experiences. With 27 species of cetacean plying Azorean waters, including sperm whales and blue whales (depending on the time of year), sightings here are guaranteed.
A World Cetacean Alliance partner dedicated to sustainable tourism, Dolphin and Whale Connection (dolphinandwhaleconnection.com) offers whale- and dolphin-watching tours.

GO

↗ SWEDEN

Widely considered to be the world's most sustainable country, Sweden almost guarantees your travel footprint will be teeny. There are over 250 Nordic Ecolabel–stamped hotels and hostels to choose from, as well as hundreds of tours with Nature's Best ecotourism certification. Buzz around Gothenburg on bicycles, explore Stockholm's urban national park, and dine on organic, locally sourced produce just about everywhere in between. *Read more about Sweden's sustainable initiatives at sweden.se/nature/sustainable-living.*

NEPAL

Travelling sustainably extends to spending your tourist dollars as thoughtfully as possible. The 7.8-magnitude earthquake that struck in April 2015 devastated Nepal's tourism industry. With most affected trekking routes now reopened and many communities reliant on income from trekking groups, there's no better time to go. *Want to stay on to help rebuild a village? Sustainable-travel company Eco Companion (ecocompanion.com) runs a 20-day program.*

GANSBAAI, SOUTH AFRICA

Recently little more than a fishing village, Gansbaai is now thriving with community-focused, responsible-tourism initiatives and activities – hike, kayak, fat bike, whale watch and more. Its Grootbos Private Nature Reserve has been a shining light, winning awards for poverty reduction and conservation of fynbos flora. *Watch whales with Dyer Island Cruises (whale watchsa.com), a Fair Trade Tourism certified company involved with conservation projects.*

CAYUGA COLLECTION HOTELS, COSTA RICA

A global leader in sustainability, Costa Rica is working to become the first carbon-neutral country by 2020. On top of the environmentally and culturally friendly attractions and tours are reams of sustainable hotels. Tucked away in incredible corners of the Costa Rican wilderness, check out the Cayuga Collection (cayugaonline.com) of eight award-winning sustainable properties. *Look for Certification for Sustainable Tourism-listed hotels, which must comply with a model of natural-, cultural- and social-resource management.*

⬉ COMMUNITY HOMESTAYS

Bedding down with a local family is a great way to learn about, and give back to, communities that may not otherwise benefit from the tourist traffic that passes through. The tricky part is ensuring that your stay benefits the community in the long term. Fortunately, many sustainable-travel operators do this groundwork for you. *Visit www.responsibletravel.com/ holidays/homestays for sustainable homestay options across the globe, from Goa to Guatemala.*

TOP
FIVE
TRENDS
BEST IN
TRAVEL
2017

DO

↗ OPT FOR ETHICAL ELEPHANT INTERACTIONS

Riding an elephant used to be a rite of passage for travellers to Thailand. Today, however, there is strong evidence to support expert claims that elephant rides and shows are harmful for these gentle giants. Fortunately, a growing number of Thai sanctuaries offer visitors the chance to interact with elephants in an environment that's safe for both parties. *Check out Elephant Nature Park (elephant naturepark.org) near Chiang Mai, and Elephants World (elephantsworld.org) near Kanchanaburi.*

SUPPORT SUSTAINABLE RESTAURANTS

From farm-to-table restaurants to reducing food loss and waste, initiatives adopted by restaurants around the world are making a difference to the planet. Cities leading the charge include Seattle, with its mandatory recyclable food containers and Copenhagen, home to many highly sustainable restaurants. *Visiting Copenhagen? Book a table at Relae (restaurant-relae.dk) or Rub & Stub (spisrubogstub.dk).*

BE CONSCIOUS OF YOUR PLASTIC FOOTPRINT

Many of the world's most popular travel destinations can't cope with the volume of waste produced by locals, let alone visitors. On the Indonesian island of Bali, for example, it's thought that around three million plastic bottles are used every month. Refill reusable canteens instead of buying plastic bottles, use cloth carry bags and avoid using plastic straws in drinks. *Visit banthebottle.com for more on the impact of plastic bottles on the environment.*

• By Sarah Reid

LEFT: GARY LATHAM © LONELY PLANET IMAGES. RIGHT: JOSEPH BRODERICK / EYEEM © GETTY IMAGES

INDEX

RIGHT: PHILIP LEE HARVEY © LONELY PLANET IMAGES

ACKNOWLEDGEMENTS

PUBLISHED IN 2016 BY LONELY PLANET GLOBAL LIMITED

CRN 554153
www.lonelyplanet.com
ISBN 978 1 7865 7115 1
© Lonely Planet 2016
© Photographs as indicated 2016
Printed in Singapore

MANAGING DIRECTOR, PUBLISHING Piers Pickard
ASSOCIATE PUBLISHER Robin Barton
COMMISSIONING EDITOR Jessica Cole
ASSISTANT EDITOR Christina Webb
ART DIRECTION Daniel Di Paolo
LAYOUT DESIGNER Austin Taylor
EDITORS Sarah Bailey, Bridget Blair
IMAGE RESEARCHER Shweta Andrews
CARTOGRAPHER Wayne Murphy
PRINT PRODUCTION Larissa Frost, Nigel Longuet

WRITTEN BY James Bainbridge, Sarah Bennett, Joe Bindloss, Jean-Bernard Carillet, Jessica Cole, Janine Eberle, Helen Elfer, Lauren Finney, Imogen Hall, Tom Hall, Paula Hardy, John Hecht, Anita Isalska, Gabrielle Jaffe, Mark Johanson, James Kay, Patrick Kinsella, Michael Kohn, Tom Masters, Lorna Parkes, Matt Phillips, Brandon Presser, Kevin Raub, Sarah Reid, Brendan Sainsbury, Daniel Savery Raz, James Smart, Regis St Louis, Phillip Tang, Tasmin Waby, Rebecca Warren, Luke Waterson, Chris Zeiher

THANKS TO Steve Handley, Flora MacQueen, Maria McKenzie

STAY IN TOUCH lonelyplanet.com/contact

AUSTRALIA The Malt Store, Level 3, 551 Swanston St, Carlton, Victoria 3053 03 8379 8000

IRELAND Unit E, Digital Court, The Digital Hub, Rainsford St, Dublin 8

USA 150 Linden St, Oakland, CA 94607 510 250 6400

UK 240 Blackfriars Rd, London SE1 8NW 020 3771 5100

MIX
Paper from
responsible sources
FSC™ C021741

Paper in this book is certified against the Forest Stewardship Council™ standards. FSC™ promotes environmentally responsible, socially beneficial and economically viable management of the world's forests.